# DANCING WITH MERCE CUNNINGHAM

-:-:-:-:-:-:-:-:-:-:-:-:-:-:-

UNIVERSITY PRESS OF FLORIDA

Florida A&M University, Tallahassee
Florida Atlantic University, Boca Raton
Florida Gulf Coast University, Ft. Myers
Florida International University, Miami
Florida State University, Tallahassee
New College of Florida, Sarasota
University of Central Florida, Orlando
University of Florida, Gainesville
University of North Florida, Jacksonville
University of South Florida, Tampa
University of West Florida, Pensacola

# DANCING WITH MERCE CUNNINGHAM

-:-:-:-:-:-:-:-:-:-:-:-:-:-

MARIANNE PREGER-SIMON

Foreword by Stuart Hodes

Afterword by Alastair Macaulay

University Press of Florida

Gainesville · Tallahassee · Tampa · Boca Raton

Pensacola · Orlando · Miami · Jacksonville · Ft. Myers · Sarasota

Photographs without credit are by Marianne Preger-Simon.

This book may be available in an electronic edition.

24   23   22   21   20   19    6   5   4   3   2   1

Library of Congress Control Number: 2018947131
ISBN 978-0-8130-6485-7

The University Press of Florida is the scholarly publishing agency for the State University System of Florida, comprising Florida A&M University, Florida Atlantic University, Florida Gulf Coast University, Florida International University, Florida State University, New College of Florida, University of Central Florida, University of Florida, University of North Florida, University of South Florida, and University of West Florida.

University Press of Florida
2046 NE Waldo Road
Suite 2100
Gainesville, FL 32609
http://upress.ufl.edu

# CONTENTS

# FOREWORD

What began as a "Junior Year in Paris" for Marianne Preger-Simon soon became a commitment to Merce Cunningham and lifelong friendship with Cunningham himself. Her memoir, in addition to offering a look at the formation of his company, yields an overwhelming impression of joy. Preger-Simon went on to dance in his troupe for ten years, leaving when she decided to have children, and remaining among his circle of friends until Cunningham died in 2009.

Taking a leave from Cornell for a year in Paris in 1948, Preger-Simon was dazzled by the rebirth of arts there, as this writer, after discharge from the Army Air Corps in 1946, was dazzled by dance in New York City. At Cornell she had studied with May Atherton, the only student ever to sue Martha Graham for what she claimed was a touch that caused her back to "go out." This resulted in an order that no teacher in the Graham School was permitted to touch a student in class. Merce Cunningham, who as far as I know never taught in the Graham School but taught in rented studios before obtaining his own NYC studio, always asked, "May I touch you?" consistent with a sensitive and gentle personality that generated Preger-Simon's lifelong devotion, not only to Merce but also to the circle who gathered about him and the dance form he originated.

The slender archive of books about Merce Cunningham will benefit by the addition of this journal-like volume—journal-like because Preger-Simon did not actually keep a journal until 1957—but it draws upon letters, conversations, a good memory, and a warm relationship with and intense love for the famed choreographer.

She writes:

> Cunningham did not use dance technique. He taught it so others could produce his moves, but did not use it because he did not need it. . . . Merce created this wonderful technique for us to learn that he never used because he just WAS.

Actually Cunningham had studied tap, classical ballet, and Graham technique, teaching the last when I took his classes in 1947. But if the goal of dance technique is to free you to move as your imagination directs, Cunningham achieved it to an extraordinary degree. I can think of only one other dancer, Carmen de LaVallade, who, to cite critic Clive Barnes, "dances like the birds sing."

Preger-Simon toured with Cunningham in the days when the entire troupe, dancers, musicians, stage manager, and lighting designer toured in one VW microbus. I recall him saying, "We are quite happy at fifty miles an hour."

Stuart Hodes

# PREFACE

One day, about five or six years ago, I was examining the contents of long-unvisited boxes in the attic. I came across one box with journals dating to 1957, as well as letters I'd written to a college friend and to my parents as far back as 1948. Fortunately, my wise friend had sent me back the packet of letters I'd mailed her from France in 1948–1949 when I met Merce Cunningham, and my parents had returned to me letters I'd written to them in the 1950s when I was dancing in Merce Cunningham's company.

This electrifying treasure prompted me to ponder the possibility of writing a book about meeting Merce Cunningham, studying dance with him, dancing in his first company, and my ongoing connection to him throughout his life. Part of the book is from my memory, as unfortunately I lacked the foresight to keep a journal at first. I did start to keep a journal in 1957, during the last year I danced in the company. Over several years, as the book unfolded, it became clear that it was a personal story, full of memories, and so I included the culture that surrounded me as I encountered and participated in it. Writing this book, and looking back over so many years, has been very enjoyable and often surprisingly informative. I feel deeply blessed by the connections and events that serendipity has offered me.

There are some extended journal entries, several of which quote Merce and John Cage and others. I have also included letters and postcards I wrote to my college friend while I was in Paris, as well as to my parents during the Cunningham company's first tour on the West Coast in the fall of 1955. In several places I insert journal entries out of chronological order as a way of illustrating significant points I'm making. I've edited the entries where they are unclear, confusing or too sketchy. I've also included photos and copies of some of the many loving postcards and letters Merce sent me over the years, all of which I treasure.

What follows is a very personal picture of some grand creative artists, sifted through the memory of someone who loved them all.

# PART I

-:-:-:-:-:-:-:-:-:-:-:-:-:-

# ENTERING THE ORBIT

# 1

-:-:-:-:-:-:-:-:-:-:-:-:-:-:-:-:-

# AT THE END

"Merce would like to speak with you and Carolyn," said a smiling administrator of the Merce Cunningham Dance Company. The company was performing at Jacob's Pillow, in western Massachusetts, that July weekend in 2009. I was deeply moved that Merce wanted to say "Good-bye" to me, knowing as I did, as he did, that he was "wavering on the perimeter"(1)[1] of his phenomenal life. The administrator led Carolyn Brown and me down the aisle of the main theater to the front of the orchestra pit. A camera had been set up, this July evening, to transmit the company's performance to its failing choreographer, home in bed in New York City.

"Hi, Merce, I'm delighted to talk with you." "How good to see you, Marianne," came his warm reply.

"I hope no one drops a smoking ball into the orchestra pit to-night," I teased, recalling an incident from an early Jacob's Pillow performance that Merce loved to remind me of. (I was the horri-fied miscreant. My task had been to balance on my hand a ball with smoke emerging from it, while moving down to the front of the stage. I dropped it!) He laughed, as I'd hoped he would. We exchanged a few more words and then, "I love you, Merce, enjoy the performance." Four days later, he died. What a blessing to be able to say "Good-bye" in such a loving exchange and familiar setting.

# 2

-:-:-:-:-:-:-:-:-:-:-:-:-

# PARIS CALLS

This story starts sixty years earlier, shortly after the cauldron of destruction that was World War II had ended. Peace was followed in the western world by an explosion of artistic creativity, first in Paris, later in New York. All the collective energy and attention that had been directed toward winning the war were now available for personal creativity and individual exploration.

Drawn by the excitement and fervor of Paris, a young generation of students and artists of all persuasions poured into the city's winding streets and inexpensive hotels and garrets. An exchange rate of three hundred francs to the dollar made a year of life in France cost about the equivalent of one or two months in America. How gracious and inviting was that!

I was twenty years old when I first met Merce in 1949, near the end of my transformative year in Paris, attending Éducation par le Jeu Dramatique (ÉPJD—Education through Dramatic Play), the drama school founded by the radical and influential director/actor

Jean-Louis Barrault. I had come to Paris in 1948, after two years at Cornell University, with the intention of taking part in the Junior Year Abroad program at the Sorbonne, sponsored by Sweetbriar College. That intention was radically altered within a month after my arrival.

# 3

-:-:-:-:-:-:-:-:-:-:-:-:-

# A NEW WORLD

I traveled to France on the SS *America,* along with a friend from Cornell and a band of delightful new young international acquaintances whom I met on board and became close to during the seven-day voyage. One new friend was Hector Tosar, a Uruguayan, who was employed to play piano with a band every night of the voyage. Later on, in Uruguay, he became a celebrated pianist and composer of serial music, a twelve-tone form of composition. He taught music, was president of several musical organizations, and was exiled for ten years during the Uruguayan military dictatorship. He then returned to Uruguay with honor when the dictatorship was overturned. Like the rest of us, he was drawn to the charisma and creative energy of Paris.

We had several hours of a stopover at Southampton, England, before crossing the English Channel. I and my band of new friends struck up a conversation with the dock workers far below, flirtatious and almost inaudible. Suddenly one of them disappeared and

Off to France. Photograph by Paul Preger, my brother.

At dinner on the boat to Paris, August 1948. I'm second from right. Photographer unknown.

reappeared in our midst several minutes later, doubtless attracted to the bevy of maidens trying to interact with him and his pals. I was completely tongue-tied—he was the handsomest man I'd ever encountered. Besides, he spoke in a dialect that was incomprehensible to us. But what a great adventure. I wrote home that I'd finally met Apollo!

Selections from my first letter on arriving in France, September 2, 1948:

Well—I'm here and it is unbelievable and wonderful. . . . We got off [the boat] Wed. morning—that was very exciting and I was exploding all the time. We got on our boat train and just like in the movies all the officials and workers and passengers were screaming at each other. I found all my stuff and established myself in my compartment. There were 3 French women there, one of whom began to berate Roosevelt and his program to weaken Europe [!]—all in French and I understood her.

The Normandy countryside is just beautiful. Le Havre was much destroyed by bombs but further in it is whole. The houses are built of multicolored brick and stone and the fields are all colors and the eaves are very low and straw roofs and browsing cattle and horses and one or two goats peering out of the foliage. Then there are towns where colored roofs are all in a bunch. All kinds of color all over and very verdant growth and beautifully cultivated farms with old barn-homes. The Normans are VERY tight. . . .

Then we came near Paris and then saw the Tour Eiffel and then we were in the Gare St. Lazare [railroad station]. . . . drove here via the Champs-Elysées . . . then we came up on an astonishing elevator without a top and very tiny. Mme. Gille is charming and speaks so I can understand her. I have a room with French windows that open on a court and you can hear people through the court—it's lovely. The living room opens (little balcony) on trees and a beautiful street and you can see the Tour Eiffel from it. Then I took a walk around for an hour—saw Les Invalides so beautiful with a great garden in front—and the Rue Lecourbe around here which has stores and street wagons with food. And narrow streets with tremendous colors on the stone of the houses and in the fancy signs on the narrow 18th century stores—Ohhh—it's soo [sic] exciting. And everyone carries huge loaves of bread unwrapped.

Then she [Mme. Gille] served tea and bread and butter and I met her daughter Nicole who is very charming, sensitive and intelligent and speaks also wery well and slowly enough for me. Everyone is so nice.

This morning . . . she [Mme. Gille] wheeled in my breakfast to my room—toast and a great bowl of tea—not a cup but a bowl. . . . I met Nicole as I was strolling—the outside market where all the merchants shout what they are selling and how much—so colorful.

We had lunch—Papa comes home—he is small, moustached, and very nice and very French. We had raw artichokes! and wine and steak, potatoes, lettuce, cheese (delicious) and the beautiful French bread—brown.

Then Nicole and I went to the Comédie Française and saw Marivaux and Molière—Le Médecin Malgré Lui—and I learned about the Métro. Then we walked past the Louvre and through the Tuileries [garden]—my God so gorgeous with a billion flowers. And along the Seine to the Quais to the Trocadéro for a view of Paris. It is breathtaking and better than all imagination. Every time you look there is a beautiful building or monument or flowers, or a charming street or something wonderful.

Nicole is . . . charming, serene and lovely and mature . . .

Meals are like a Bonnard: plaid cloth, next to a French window and wonderful view, jug of wine and of water, basket of brown bread and everything served one by one, not together like us. I LOVE IT.

I am thrilled by everything—everyone is so cordial and helpful and PARIS is magnificent.

I had arranged to live with a wonderful French family that was also boarding two lovely students from California. The Gille family lived in a large apartment building in Montparnasse, a section of Paris on the left bank of the Seine River. The apartment building was located on a broad handsome avenue that led to the Eiffel Tower at its far end. The father, Pierre Gille, was a banker. He was more conservative than the rest of his family, seemed proper, kindly and looked exactly like my idea of a Frenchman—short, trim, with a mustache. The mother of the family, Simone Gille-Delafon, his wife, was a sturdy, vigorous, outgoing woman. She was an important critic for the journal, *Les Arts*. She was definitely in charge of the family, and of the three American girls she was responsible for. Her sense of responsibility came to the fore in two incidents that I remember. The first was when I showed up at dinner after school one evening with the slang, and its accompanying accent, that I had picked up from my young classmates. Madame Gille was horrified and let me know that it was not welcome in their home. Her job was to make sure that her American girls spoke perfect upper class French. This was an excellent lesson in Situational Behavior, which I absorbed rapidly. Slang in school, eloquence at the Gilles' home.

My second lesson came after I had invited my American friend, Arthur Polonsky, to the house. We went into my room and closed the door, so that we could chat and draw each other without interrupting anyone else. Afterward, I received a lesson about French morals: Before marriage a girl must behave with complete and total innocence around men. After marriage she could do whatever she wanted. This lesson left me with my mouth open in astonishment at the complete contrast, but I made an effort to reassure Mme. Gille that I completely understood and agreed with her.

Their son, Alain, was home for a small part of that year, and was in his early twenties. He was quite handsome, also short like his papa. I don't remember what he was doing at the time, but he went on to become a very active member of UNESCO. Nicole, their daughter, was in her mid-twenties and was a social worker. She was warm, friendly, and was my guide in my first weeks in Paris. She became my dear friend during that year, as well as for many years afterward. She resembled her father physically and was a lovely young woman.

I wrote about Madame Gille in a letter dated June 19, 1949:

There is to be a Congress of the International Association of Art Critics here this month and Madame Gille is Secretary-General. I am translating the statutes into English and she is so grateful that she has promised to take me to all the interesting events! And she has given me a permanent card to attend the plays being given in an international competition of young dramatic companies! I really have been pursued by good luck this year—and you know it doesn't come from work or worth or even aggression—it's just free.

# 4

-:-:-:-:-:-:-:-:-:-:-:-:-:-:-

# THE ART WORLD BECKONS

Madame Gille was also able to offer me the happy opportunity to attend all the art openings in Paris, including Picasso's ground-breaking first sculpture exhibit. (One time I saw Picasso running across the Champs Elysées laughing, holding hands with Françoise Gilot, his companion at the time, and in his other hand carrying a broom.)

I had an adventure at one of the openings I attended less than a month after arriving in Paris, recorded in this letter to a friend, written in September of 1948:

> I went to a gallery exhibit opening the other day, and an
> elegant lady and gentleman stopped me. He was a painter
> [named Berea] and thought I looked like a Renoir and
> wanted to paint me! I went to his studio—with a friend, of
> course—what a palace! It's tremendous, with a very high
> ceiling and a huge window—every artist's dream. Some of his

paintings are quite good, some are frightful. He is a society painter—has exhibited in some of the sweller galleries and has done lots of portraits of famous people. He started a painting of me, but if it doesn't improve I shall resign and look for a better artist.

A detail not mentioned in the letter: My Boston artist friend Michael Tulysewski, in Paris on a scholarship, declared quite firmly that he would accompany me to the sittings in Berea's studio. He would draw me also. Apparently he was less naive than I. Monsieur Berea agreed to the arrangement rather reluctantly. The end result was that Berea's portrait was quite mediocre (he insisted that he was distracted by Michael's presence), whereas Michael made a large exquisite pencil drawing, which currently hangs in our living room. Despite the inadequacy of Berea's portrait, he included it in a one-man show later that year.

Although I didn't know it at the time, Dimitrie Berea was already a much admired Postimpressionist painter, and went on to become both successful and famous. He was born in Romania, came to Paris to live and paint and was friends with Picasso, Matisse, Bonnard, and others of his contemporaries. In the sixties, he came to the United States, married a Romanian ex-pat, Princess Alice Gureilli, and continued his successes until he died. His wife established a gallery in his name at Berea College in Kentucky. She felt the name of the college was a sign that her husband's paintings should be there in a gallery entirely dedicated to his works. The gallery contains many of his paintings. Others are owned by collectors, galleries, and museums around the world.

Actually, Berea College is remarkable. It was founded in 1855 by an abolitionist and was the first interracial and coeducational college in the South. Tuition was completely covered for every student, and still is. It was named after a biblical town of open-minded citizens.

Michael Tulysewski made this pencil drawing of me in Paris in 1948.

# 5

-:-:-:-:-:-:-:-:-:-:-:-:-:-:-

# POSTWAR REVERBERATIONS

Life in the Gille household, as in all of Paris, was still deeply affected by the deprivations of the war. There was food rationing, and there was a unique natural refrigeration: The kitchen had a wide cupboard built into the wall of the house. The cupboard doors opened to the kitchen, but the back of the cupboard was a mesh grate that was open to the outside, so that food put into the cupboard was exposed to the outside air. That was how food was kept cool. I have no idea what they did in the summer! But the lack of real refrigeration required food shopping every day in the outdoor market down the street.

In France, everyone drank wine at meals. Children drank water that had a bit of wine in it, so that they felt like they were given what the adults had. The Gilles gave the three young Americans wine to drink, but discovered that one of them—me—got slightly sozzled after two sips of wine, so I was treated like the children and had my

Vin du Portugal (that was the only wine available) well diluted. That saved my sanity.

One of the amazing things I learned from Nicole, the twenty-five-year-old daughter of the family, was that during the war she, her mother, and her younger brother, Alain, all worked in the Underground (actively against the Nazi occupation), but they never knew that each other was part of it until after the war. They had an astonishing and life-preserving ability to keep secrets.

# 6

-:-:-:-:-:-:-:-:-:-:-:-

# SERENDIPITY OPENS A NEW DOOR

Nicole took me on a tour of Paris shortly after I arrived. Among the many places we visited was a class in mask-making, at ÉPJD, Éducation par le Jeu Dramatique (Education through Dramatic Play), also located in Montparnasse. I decided the drama school was a much more intriguing way to use my time than the Sorbonne. As I wrote home in a letter, I would be meeting "real French kids" instead of international students. My father, back home in New York, replied to my request to make the switch in plans with kindly irony: "You're three thousand miles away and there's nothing I can do about it, so go ahead." It turned out to be the best fatherly advice I could have received.

The postwar artistic ferment in Paris was shared by the theater community. Several great theater directors were bursting with fascinating offerings. In addition to Barrault, there were Charles Dullin, Jean Vilar, and Louis Jouvet, all mounting brilliant, newly envisioned productions of both new and familiar plays. Part of the blessing of studying at ÉPJD was receiving free tickets to the openings of some of these performances. Three of the plays stand out in my memory: *Les Fourberies de Scapin*, by Molière, a takeoff on the Italian Commedia dell'Arte, starring Jean-Louis Barrault and directed by Louis Jouvet, with decor and costumes by Christian Bérard. As I wrote to a friend:

> Went to the opening of Barrault's latest play, *Les Fourberies de Scapin*, by Molière. It was attended by all the celebrities and titles and elegances which inhabit Paris, and they were an exquisite sight to see, in evening dress and chauffeur (all borrowed from a stage prop store, no doubt). The play was excellent, directed by Louis Jouvet, which is amazing that the two greatest actors in Paris should cooperate on a play like that— a good thing. The décor was the last of Christian Bérard, who just died last week in the theater. It was splendid—all in grey and white, with rose in the background, and touches of color on the costumes, which were also grey and white.

For the theater of the time—and following the trend set by the *Ballets Russes*, which had attracted artists from a variety of fields—decors and costumes played a crucial role in theatrical productions. Christian Bérard was a fashion illustrator and designer. His drawings appeared in *Vogue* and *Harpers Bazaar*, and he illustrated the work of the leading designers of the period, including Schiaparelli. He was a luminary as well in the dance world for his costume designs for Balanchine ballets, notably *Cotillon*. He died in 1949, aged forty-seven, while preparing costumes and set for *Les Fourberies de Scapin*.

The second play that stands out in my memory was *Hamlet* in a translation by André Gide, with music by Arthur Honegger, costumes and decor by André Masson, directed by and starring Jean-Louis Barrault; I wrote to my friend: "Barrault's [recent] play was excellent. *Hamlet* is so French and more symbolic and unreal and externalized than [Laurence] Olivier's [production]. One cannot compare the two [productions of Hamlet]. I loved them both; both were masters of their particular interpretation. The translation is quite beautiful and Barrault's movement is dance!"

Jean-Louis Barrault was a tremendously gifted mime, actor, and director who had won international fame for his role as Baptiste in the movie *Children of Paradise* (1944). André Masson was already a well-established artist who had been associated with the Surrealist movement but was finding his own personal style, an echo of his experience in WWI and of his views on the Spanish civil war. He was perhaps the most inspired choice for designing *Hamlet*'s stage sets.

The *Hamlet* translation I found "so French" had in fact won high praise for the future Nobel Prize winner André Gide. After the opening, *Time* magazine had commented: "Traditionally, *Hamlet* has never fared very happily in France. Though many a good French writer has tried to translate that least Gallic of poems, the first to make a first-rate job of it was Hamlet-like André Gide. Last week Gide's translation was superbly presented on the stage. Long before all the brilliance of Paris rose to cheer the play's swift, incisive three and a half hours, it was clear that tradition was dead & buried. From now on *Hamlet* was going to be happy in Paris" (*Time*, October 28, 1948).

It was not the first time Arthur Honegger had written music for a play, and he had been already inspired by Shakespeare's *The Tempest*. But to have someone considered as the greatest musician alive in France at the time write for a new production of *Hamlet* was another sign that Jean-Louis Barrault and Gide together had achieved something no one else had done before.

The last of the three plays I so much enjoyed was *Ondine*, by Jean Giraudoux, a fantasy play about a water sprite and a human man falling in love, which was directed by Louis Jouvet—who had also the starring role—with décor by Pavel Tchelitchew. Tchelitchew had moved from Russia to Paris in 1923, and for a while was part of a band of artists that included Christian Bérard. First a Surrealist, his work would develop in different directions over many years. (He was also an important designer for Balanchine in the 1930s, both in Paris and New York. His painting "Hide and Seek" is one of the most enduringly popular holdings in the permanent collection of the Museum of Modern Art in New York.)

These three plays reunited in one way or another some of the best minds, artists, and performers of postwar France.

What good fortune I reaped being in Paris in the midst of such an explosion of productive creativity by so many remarkable artists. Paris was one of the few great European cities completely preserved from destruction during World War II by being declared an "Open City" and was saved toward the end of the war by the last Nazi governor of Paris, General Dietrich von Choltitz. He defied Hitler's orders to "Defend Paris to the last bullet or else destroy the city." I have no doubt that he fell in love with the charismatic city, as did so many brilliant artists and followers during the time I was privileged to be there.

There was also an exciting influx of renowned classical musicians, including Yehudi Menuhin, outstanding violinist, born in America, and Vladimir Horowitz, born in Ukraine and considered the greatest pianist ever, now free to play concerts around the world once again. I felt privileged to attend their performances.

One particular concert I remember, at the Salle Gaveau, was a performance of Béla Bartók's fourth quartet, composed in 1928. I was fortunate to have purchased the score in advance, so was able to follow visually what I was hearing. As a result, I had no trouble engaging fully with the music, which was considerably more complex than I was accustomed to. I find that quartet is still very familiar and easy to follow when I hear it now.

# 1

-:-:-:-:-:-:-:-:-:-:-:-:-:-

# TIES TO HOME

While I was in Paris, three American artist friends of mine were there, also.

All three were in Paris on scholarship from the Boston Museum School of Fine Arts, having just completed four years at the school. I had met all three in the summer of 1947 while attending classes of the Boston Museum School in Pittsfield, Massachusetts, after my freshman year at Cornell. Arthur Polonsky had been my painting teacher, and he soon became a very dear friend. (That summer I also became friends with Ben Shahn, a world-famous social-realist painter and photographer, who was teaching the advanced painting class. When I would meet him in the hall, I would bow reverently and say, "Master!" He would reply gravely, with a twinkling eye, "Mistress!")

One of Arthur Polonsky's friends in Boston was a young woman in her teens named Janice (I don't recall her last name) who had taken it upon herself to form a Salon consisting of the

Arthur Polonsky, the American friend who visited me in my room in Paris. He later became an important Boston Expressionist painter. Photograph taken by me in 1949.

up-and-coming Boston artists and musicians. Her mother was an inspired Jewish cook who supplied the mostly financially strapped young artists with generous helpings of fulfilling foods, making everyone very happy. Arthur invited me to one of these events. My outstanding memory from that party, aside from the delicious meal, was hearing Lukas Foss play the piano. His friends all crowded around the piano, calling out the names of different composers, requesting him to improvise music in their style, which he did brilliantly, amidst great laughter and cheers. I particularly remember his mastery of Mozart (always my favorite composer). He was truly remarkable. Born in Germany, he was quickly recognized as a child prodigy on the piano. In 1937, at age fifteen, he and his family moved to the United States, where he became close friends with Leonard Bernstein as well as a student of Sergei Koussevitzky at

Tanglewood. In addition to being a fine pianist, he was a respected composer and conductor, whose music was often played on programs featuring John Cage and Merce Cunningham. He became a professor of music, and music director of several orchestras. In the year 2000 he was awarded a gold medal by the American Academy of Arts and Letters. He lived to be eighty-six years old.

Michael Tulysewski and Diana Kelty were Arthur's very closest friends and so became mine. Michael and Arthur were part of the group of Boston Expressionists, and both had many exhibitions of their work in later years. Arthur also taught painting at Brandeis University and Boston University. His work is in many museums, as well as in public and private collections worldwide. Through them, I had met other artists in Boston who were also spending time in Paris, including Ralph Coburn and Ellsworth Kelly. Kelly's work is collected and celebrated worldwide, and commands extraordinary prices at art auctions. He became a painter, sculptor, and print-maker, associated with Hard-Edge, Color Field, and Minimalist styles. With all of these artists, our social time almost always consisted of drawing each other, drawings that I still have.

I described our Thanksgiving celebration in a letter written shortly afterward—this one about food:

Thanksgiving was splendid. At 1 PM I went out to search for a raw turkey and returned at 4 PM successful. I made stuffing here out of all sorts of wonderful things, stuffed the turkey and took it to a baker who did a gorgeous job roasting it (we have no oven). I took it then to Michael's room and Polonsky, Michael, another Boston artist, [Ellsworth] Kelly, a Chinese musician, a female Palestinian pianist, and another American girl, and I had a huge banquet of roast turkey, champagne and fruit . . . Everyone was crazy with joy over the unexpected celebration, Polonsky and the Chinese boy played violin and piano duets, and the Palestinian girl played some piano solos. It was a wonderful evening.

Michael Tulysewski and Diana Kelty, close friends of mine and Arthur's in Paris. Photographer unknown.

Drawing of me by Ellsworth Kelly, Paris, dated January 23, 1949.

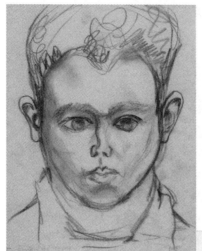

*Left*: My drawing of Ellsworth Kelly, Paris, also dated January 23, 1949.

*Below*: And my drawing of Arthur Polonsky, Paris, bearing the same date.

*Bottom*: Arthur's drawing of Michael Tulysewski and Diana Kelty— undated, but probably Paris, 1949.

$8$

-:-:-:-:-:-:-:-:-:-:-:-

# ONE STEP LEADS TO ANOTHER

Into this artistic commotion that was freeing invention and challenging convention, came Merce Cunningham and John Cage, adept at both those cultural shifts.

In late spring of 1949, I learned that Merce Cunningham was giving a dance concert in the studio of a leading modernist, later figurative artist, Jean Hélion, in Paris.

I had seen Merce's phenomenal aerial performance in *Letter to the World*, as part of Martha Graham's company, several years before I left the States, and admired his dancing enormously, so I made a point of being at the studio event. I found this concert very exciting. Merce's dancing and his choreography were radically different from Graham's, differences that I would understand more fully as I became his student. I expressed my enthusiasm in a letter to a friend, written July 15, 1949 (I apparently melded together the studio performance and the brief performance a month later, part of a multi-person event at the Théâtre du Vieux Colombier):

Merce danced the other night—my goodness, I have never seen anything like him in my life. He gives the impression of never being static, but of never making an effort—a continuous, completely unified flow, like the song of a bird—he makes all movements—angular, curved, moments of no movement—anything you want—but the unity and lucidity are so complete—and he has such a perfect understanding and use of space, of his body, of time—it's really terribly exciting and moving—I didn't breathe all the way through. That was a solo [I believe it was *Root of an Unfocus*]. Then he did two trios [actually one trio, *Effusions Avant l'Heure*[1] and a duet, *Amores*, with Le Clercq] with two women—ballet dancers [Tanaquil Le Clercq and Betty Nichols, both members of the New York City Ballet]—that were in between ballet and modern. Those I liked less because of the ballet principle involved—of static "tableaux"—I always feel that those tableaux are so gratuitous—no reason for them or connection with what follows. But there, too, the movement patterns were exquisite. He really conquers the dimensions in his choreography. And such a fluid body;—a formidable technique, that is so good it becomes secondary in the dance, and the whole thing enters through the observer's stomach without need of an intellectual interpretation or assimilation.

I suspect that my discomfort with the "static 'tableaux'" was less about "ballet principles" than about early indications of Merce's interest in stillness as part of movement, which remarkably distinguished him from so many other contemporary choreographers. I later came to value and appreciate the stillness in such dances as *Septet* and *Springweather and People*.

What is interesting to me is that what I was perceiving with so much delighted excitement as a member of the audience, was being experienced as rather chaotic from the point of view of one of the dancers, Betty Nichols.

The artist Jean Hélion's studio in Paris. It was here that I first saw Merce dance his own choreography. Photographer unknown.

Here is her description of the making and performance of Merce's dance concert, excerpted from an interview with Ballet Review:

Nichols: 1949 was a fantastic year in Paris. Everything was happening. Everybody was there. It was recovering from the war fast.

Tanny [Tanaquil Le Clercq] and I had been in Paris a week. We were walking on the pavé of St. Chapelle and heard "Betty! Tanny!" We turned; it was Merce Cunningham and John Cage. "We're going to have a recital. You've got to do it with us." I knew Merce because he was at SAB [School of American Ballet]. He took class. I didn't know him personally, but Tanny had danced Merce's *Seasons* at Ballet Society.

The Cage music was very difficult. I remember being terrified because he gave us such liberty—already—that I said, "I'm never going to know when to come in."

"That's all right, that's all right," Merce said. "You'll find it." But I was never sure. I don't think I was doing it the same each time.

BR: He didn't care.

Nichols: Exactly, it didn't seem to matter. At that time I didn't know anything about that. Maybe even Merce didn't. Maybe that was just beginning. We had ballet shoes and we wore rehearsal clothes. We had tights and a sweater. Pat McBride's mother used to knit these sweaters for dancers.

It was done in the painter Jean Hélion's studio. There was tremendous publicity about the program. It was the first time Paris had ever seen anything like that, and it was so astounding that they didn't know how to criticize it. So what they said was—they always fall back on this when they can't think of anything else—"It was so beautiful." Giacometti was there, and Alice B. Toklas. *Le tout Paris* came [meaning, everybody who was notable].

I was impressed by the elegance of both Nichols and Le Clercq and visually aware of their ballet training from the way they moved. However, as my letter indicates, Merce's performance overwhelmed every other impression, and became the complete focus of my attention. Furthermore, balletic movement was familiar to me, whereas his personal style was so new and electric.

Ralph Coburn, who was also at the concert, told me that he and his friend Ellsworth Kelly, Merce Cunningham, and John Cage, the composer, were staying in the same hotel, the Hotel de Bourgogne on the Ile St. Louis. He informed me that Merce was looking for a studio to work in.

That was all the encouragement I needed. Several days later I sat outside the hotel until Merce came out, then accosted him and

Ludolf Schild dancing with Jacqueline Levant, perhaps in 1946–1947. I studied dance with her; it was thanks to her that Merce began to teach in Paris. Photographer unknown.

informed him that I knew of a studio where he could work and also teach a class.

Part of the curriculum of ÉPJD had been a dance class held in studio 121 at the Salle Pleyel, originally taught by the gifted German modern dancer, Ludolf Schild, student of Mary Wigman and familiar with Martha Graham's work. I described my first sight of Schild in a letter from October 1948:

My goodness was I shocked. I'd expected, for some reason, an older man. Instead appeared this magnificent looking young man. He has great troughs in his cheeks, and deep-set burning eyes, and he's long and thin. He has a small beard all around the edge of his jaw—just beautiful. He walks with a cane because of an operation he had last year . . . Everyone hopes he will be able to dance again. At one point after class, he stood in front of a mirror with his cane and, with an ironic smile, said, "Voilà, le danseur Schild" [There is the dancer, Schild]. Then he turned and saw my long face and said, "C'est triste, eh?" [It's sad, eh?]. And it was—not only because it would be horrible not to be able to dance again, but also because he would die in his soul if he were to become bitter as a result.

Schild died of cancer in early June 1949. His classes had been taken over by his protégée, Jacqueline Levant, when he became too sick to teach. Jacqueline had been his devoted dance partner, collaborator, and lover. She was interested in having important guests teaching in studio 121. She assured me she'd be happy to have Merce teach there, so she could learn from another master. (She went on to teach at ÉPJD for three more years, and to perform in the Ballets Modernes de Paris from 1953 to 1955.) This was all amicably arranged, and so began my life in the orbit of Merce Cunningham.

Here is an account of my meeting with Merce, from a letter I wrote to a friend on June 19, 1949:

Merce Cunningham is here and I met him last week—spent an hour talking to him, discussing dance, theatre, etc. I was able to give various information he's been searching for since arriving. Yesterday, he came to my school to see our mime course, and was very enthusiastic and interested, and kept whispering observations and comments to me throughout. He is an angel—charming and so interested/interesting. And he is teaching all summer here beginning Tuesday!! At last, after eight months I can really dance—and with *him*! Imagine. I'm exploding with joy—how I've missed dancing—it's surprising, considering what a new acquaintance it is.

Dancing was indeed a new acquaintance of mine. When I first arrived at Cornell in 1946, I developed a strained achilles tendon in one leg from walking up and down the hilly streets of Ithaca. When the college doctor helped me into a small whirlpool foot bath, he said, "You should dance. You have such flexible feet." So I thought, "Yes, what a nice idea!" and joined the Dance Club, led by a Graham-trained dancer, May Atherton. As I later discovered, flexible feet were definitely not one of my major assets—but I'm eternally grateful for his incorrect analysis. It pushed me into a splendid world.

May Atherton had been trained by Martha Graham. When I joined the Dance Club at Cornell in 1946, she—looking just like this—was my dance teacher. I studied with her three semesters in 1947–1948. Photo: Wesp-Buzzell, Inc.

# 9

-:-:-:-:-:-:-:-:-:-:-:-:-:-

# ANOTHER CHERISHED
# NEW FRIEND

I also attended Merce's second performance at the Théâtre du Vieux Colombier, on the left bank of the Seine River, July 11, 1949. My beloved teacher at ÉPJD, the innovative director/actor Roger Blin, was on the same program. He was to be responsible for introducing the plays of Samuel Beckett to France, beginning in 1953. A small theater at the Théâtre de l'Odéon has been dedicated to him: the Salon Roger Blin.

Roger Blin, too, had made a great impression on me, as I wrote in a letter after meeting him for the first time:

> I have a new god to worship. His name is Blin. He wears knickers and wonderful colors and has wild hair and is beautiful.

CLUB D'ESSAI

de la

- RADIODIFFUSION FRANÇAISE -

-:-:-:-:-:-:-:-:-:-:-:-:-:-:-

SOIREE DE L'IMPREVU

-:-:-:-:-:-:-:-:-:-:-:-:-:-:-

PRODUCTION : André FREDERIQUE

REALISATION : Jacques REYNIER

---------------------

THEATRE DU VIEUX COLOMBIER

LUNDI 11 JUILLET 1949

-:-:-:-:-:-:-:-:-:-:-

---

PREMIERE PARTIE
-:-:-:-:-:-:-:-:-:-

-OUVERTURE - ( Orchestre Pierre DEVEVEY)

- PRESENTATION DU SPECTACLE
  Pierre DUMAYET et Roland DUBILLARD

- CINQ MINUTES DE MAUVAISE MUSIQUE (Pierre BARBAUD)
  Orchestre Pierre DEVEVEY

-PORTRAITS HISTORIQUES
  Roger PIERRE et Alain BOUVETTE

- MELODIES
  a) au pays de la Magie ... H. Michaux -M.Leroux
  b) Sanglots .............. Apollinaire-Poulenc
  c) Offrande ............. Anonyme XIIIé -Poulenc
  (extrait des "Chansons Gaillardes)

- TCHITCHIKOF et KOROBOTCHKA .... Nicolas GOGOL
  avec François VIBERT et la voix de Marguerite MORENO
  extrait de l'enregistrement des "Ames Mortes"
  adaptation de Pierre Brive - mise en ondes de
  Maurice CAZENEUVE - Présentation scénique de
  Jacques REYNIER

- LES ENTRETIENS DE LA BELLE ET DE LA BETE (Ravel)
  Marionnettes à main nue animées par O'BRADY

- NON -LIEU - Henri CALET -
  La Compagnie les "Argonautes"
  dirigée par Sylvain DHOMME

          Germaine LECOYER
          Philippe KELLERSON
          Etienne BIERRY
          Reine COURTOIS
          Robert POSTEK
          Paul CHEVALIER

-MELODIES
  a) Das Marienleben ..........Paul Hindemith
  b)Air Italien
  c) Los Disparts ............. Desnos-Poulenc
  d) Air populaire américain

          Ethel BOYD accompagnée au piano par
                              Thomas GOODMAN

---

## 2

- LE PROCES DE CHRISTOPHE-COLOMB ( Ph. de CHERISEY)

par la Compagnie Michel de RE

          Monique LENIER
          Philippe de CHERISEY
          Pierre TCHERNIA
          Georges LAUNAY
          Solange CERTAIN
          Jacques JEANNET
          Michel de RE

Choeur et orchestre sous la direction
de Pierre DEVEVEY

-------------------------------

E N T R ' A C T E
-------------------------------

DEUXIEME PARTIE
-:-:-:-:-:-:-:-:-:-:-:-

-OUVERTURE A LA FRANCAISE ( André HODEIR)
  Orchestre Pierre DEVEVEY

- TEXTES INEDITS ....... Antonin ARTAUD
  mis en scène par Yves LE GALL
  interprétés par Paule THEVENIN, Roger BLIN
                          et Maurice PETIPAS

- TROIS DANSES ........... John CAGE
  interprétées par Betty NICHOLS, Merce CUNNINGHAM
  et Tanagrit LE CLERCQ
  Au piano préparé : John CAGE

- ESSAI nº 3 SUR LA SOLIDARITE HUMAINE (Bert. BRECHT)
  mise en scène par Yves LE GALL
  avec les voix de Camille BRYEN, André FREDERIQUE
  Mousi LANTI, Bernard AMOUROUX et Yves DARBON

---

## 3

-DEUX PIANOS
  - 194 variations sur un thème suisse
                              ( C. Saint-Saëns)
  - Samba ( extrait de
    Scaramouche) ............Darius Milhaud
    par Eveline CHAUFOUR et Claude BERARD

- CONFERENCE SUR LES LOCOMOTIVES ( André FREDERIQUE)
  mise en scène de Yves LE GALL
  avec Mousi LANTI, Claude CARNOT, Yves DARBON
  Jean GILLIBERT et Gobelins 32-08 dans le rôle
                              du père -

- AGNES CAPRI
  a) Rengaine à pleurs ..J. Tardieu-M.Karveno
  b) Le Même Néant ...... Jean Tardieu
  c) l'espèce humaine.... Raymond Queneau
  d) Criné .............. Max Jacob-Rietti
  e) Dans les appartements de
     la reine ............ Henri Michaux
  f) Ophélie ............. Agnès Capri
                          Christiane Verger
  accompagnée au piano par Hubert DEGEX

- CHARIVARI COMIQUE
  par Roland DUBILLARD et Pierre DUMAYET

- UNE HEURE AVEC ..... Marcel CERDAN
  par Frédéric LEFEVRE

- L'AUTEUR AU THEATRE ( Max JACOB)

  mise en scène Michel de RE
  avec Malène MARCOUSSIS , Solange CERTAIN,
  Philippe de CHERISEY, Pierre TCHERNIA
  Georges LAUNAY, Michel de RE, Jacques JEANNET
  Choeur et orchestre sous la direction de
                      Pierre DEVEVEY

- ESSAI DE FINALE par ..... le Public

          Régie : Gilles de FREITAS

          -:-:-:-:-:-:-:-:-

---

The program for the Théâtre du Vieux Colombier, performance of July 11, 1949. This featured two of the men who became my gods in Paris: Merce Cunningham and the actor-director Roger Blin.

Roger Blin, actor, director, teacher, and friend. Photographer unknown.

In a later letter, June 19, 1949, I wrote about becoming friends with him:

> You remember I mentioned away back the actor-director Roger Blin, who used to be my teacher and who inspired me with a great crush—well we have become great friends—I went to see his play [it was *La Lune dans le Fleuve Jaune (The Moon in the Yellow River)*, by Dennis Johnston, directed by Roger Blin] once a week for four weeks in a row—in order to be invited by him after to come to La Coupole [a legendary cafe in Montparnasse, famous hangout for artists of all kinds] for coffee with him and his friends. Last night was the fourth—and after his friends left, he gave me his Inside Story

over a coffee sundae. He talked for about half an hour and I listened sympathetically—you know "yes," "no," smile, etc. It was fascinating—he is such an interesting person—and a moral artist who won't compromise and as a result is tearing his heart out. An extremely sensitive and intelligent person. What a life I'm finding in Paris—I've learned so much.

One curious aspect of Blin was an intense stammer in his daily speech, which completely disappeared when he was acting a part on stage.

# 10

-:-:-:-:-:-:-:-:-:-:-:-:-:-:-

# RETURN TO NEW YORK CITY

In September 1949, I sailed to New York City on a freighter carrying champagne and artichoke hearts along with ten passengers. We encountered the tail end of a hurricane mid-Atlantic, dropped anchor, and waited it out. We were also privileged to watch in awe as the full moon rose out of the ocean. What magnificence. Ten days later we arrived safely and on time in New York, where I would now be living.

My new apartment was on the second floor of a brownstone on Jane Street, near Eighth Avenue, in Greenwich Village. It consisted of one comfortably sized room with a kitchenette and a bathroom, for the extravagant price of twenty-five dollars a month. I was very excited to have my own apartment; and the extra plus was that my beloved brother, Paul, who was getting his Master's degree at Columbia University, had another one-room apartment on the first floor. In time, I acquired two cats. My drawing of them hangs in my bedroom.

Me between Tony Franciosa (*left*) and Ben Gazzara, two new friends from the Dramatic Workshop at the New School for Social Research, New York. Photograph: Rachel Rosenthal.

Instead of continuing at Cornell, I had decided to attend the Dramatic Workshop of the New School for Social Research, headed by the German director Erwin Piscator. Piscator had come to America in 1939 and was immediately asked to create a drama school by the president of the New School for Social Research. In Germany, Piscator had developed a political style called Epic Theatre, along with Bertolt Brecht. When I arrived, the Dramatic Workshop was in the Bowery in downtown New York City, but in the spring it moved uptown to West Forty-Eighth Street, into a building that contained the President Theatre. Among my new classmates, two became close friends: Tony Franciosa and Ben Gazzara. Both went on to study at the Actor's Studio, under Elia Kazan, and appeared in movies and on Broadway. In late spring we three performed in Molière's *The Misanthrope* directed by Rachel Rosenthal, my close friend from ÉPJD. She had also returned to her family home on Central Park South in New York City, in the fall of 1949, and joined me at the Dramatic Workshop. We performed that play at the President Theatre.

*The Misanthrope*, President Theatre, New York, 1950, directed by Rachel Rosenthal. *Left to right:* me, Tony Franciosa, Ben Gazzara. Photographer unknown.

I had quite an adventure, early on in the Dramatic Workshop. One of the teachers announced that they were looking for someone to play guitar and sing a song in their next play. With no hesitation, I, who had never played guitar and had no experience singing, volunteered. I immediately went to my grandmother, who was an operatic singer and owned an 1897 lady's Martin guitar, and asked for her guidance. She taught me basic guitar chords, gave me her Martin, and wished me luck. It worked—I actually succeeded.

Rachel Rosenthal, my close friend in both Paris and New York, photographed by me, April 1950.

# 11

-:-:-:-:-:-:-:-:-:-:-:-:-:-

## DANCING

By the end of the summer, Merce had also returned to New York. He decided to start teaching his own class. He found a studio in Greenwich Village; over the years that I was dancing with him, he had several different studios, all in the same general area. He wanted to develop a technique that would train dancers to move in the way he moved so naturally.

And yet, as time passed, I was interested to observe that Merce himself never danced with any "technique." I described his style in a Dance Critics Panel June 16, 1984:[1]

> One of the things that has always struck me is that the technique that Merce developed was really developed for his dancers and he never used it. He was like Athena emerging full-blown from Zeus' head. He danced; and we learned the technique and did what we were given to do. The way

he moves is really different from the way the dancers in his company move, and yet his technique was derived from the way he danced, and the way he wanted to create dances. But he never looked like anybody else in the company when he danced. He looked like a gazelle or a lily blooming in the field or whatever. But not like somebody who had developed a great technique and was using it.

I offered a similar description at the SUNY Festival panel, March 7, 1987:[2]

> Merce created this wonderful technique for us to learn, that he never used because he just WAS. We learned the technique to approximate what he did intuitively. I always found that fascinating, because when you saw him perform a solo, it was really different from anything we did as a group. The solo was this creature, just being. We, on the other hand, were dancing [using the technique he'd taught us].

We, his students, however, worked as hard as we could to master his technique, in the determined effort to perform his class "combinations" with some fluency. Those combinations were always just beyond what we could do, producing ample frustration as well as very gradual progress. As time passed, we became aware that these challenging combinations served as opportunities for Merce to try out parts of dances he was choreographing; to see how they looked on dancers in training, as opposed to how they felt and looked on him, which was assuredly quite different.

My concern was always to dance his combinations, and his choreography, with movements as full, accurate, and rhythmically precise as possible. When I came close to achieving that, I felt transformed and deeply satisfied. I don't believe it ever occurred to me to want to be given the remarkably complex material that he performed so brilliantly. What he did, and how he did it, were unique to his spirit and his body.

The technique he was developing differed vastly from the Graham style, which was very current at the time. I'd had an earlier experience with Martha Graham's style at a holiday series of her classes that I decided to take when I was still attending Cornell University. My most vivid memory of her class was the time she asked us all to do a contraction while in a sitting position. She came over to me, pushed my head further down toward my tummy, and intoned, "Look in, look in!!" My desire in dancing was to look out, not in, which really predicted how receptive I would be to Merce's distinctive style.

In his first class I was the only student. The major rhythmical accompaniment to the exercises in the class, then and for a number of years later, was Merce's finger-snapping, persistent, commanding.

At the end of the class, he said, "Get into second position." I did. "Now plié and jump." I managed the plié, but then got stuck and couldn't move. So he came up behind me and lifted me up in the air, releasing me from my earthbound dilemma. My body got the message and I managed to jump quite successfully after that—an unforgettable entry into an aerial world.

Merce's physique was as remarkable as his dancing. He was a perfect example of "a long drink of water." He was tall, probably about six feet, and narrow. He gave the impression of having shoulders not much broader than his pelvis, though that was an illusion. He had a close-cropped mop of curly light brown hair and an attractive, expressive face, though he was far from being an open book—except when performing. In performance, his face was quite expressive, remarkably so, but it was not only his face. The movement of his head was expressive: the pace at which he moved it, the angle at which he held it. All that was so deliberate and focused that it communicated volumes—volumes that were interpreted by audience members into their own private and particular stories. In class, his manner varied according to his moods. He was very observant and would occasionally correct us. He also let us struggle a lot, wanting us to

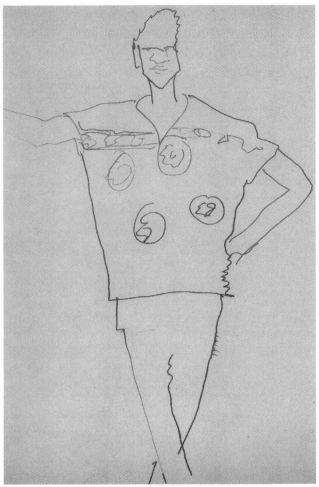

Merce, as drawn by me, around 1954.

find our way as much as possible. He would demonstrate what he wanted us to learn and do, but he didn't give a lot of verbal instructions. He seemed pleased that most of us, including me, also took ballet classes at the Metropolitan Opera Ballet School (he had studied ballet for several years at the School of American Ballet, after arriving in New York) and didn't seem to worry about what other classes we took or what other companies we danced with. (For a short period of time, I danced with both Iris Mabry, whom I had met in Paris, for two performances in June 1950 and Judith Martin for a performance in November 1952 and two more in April and May of 1953. Judith Martin was a performer, a choreographer, and cofounder of the Paper Bag Players with Remy Charlip.)

# 12

-:-:-:-:-:-:-:-:-:-:-:-:-

## WE BEGINNERS

After the first few classes, several other eager beginning students joined me, including Remy Charlip, soon to be a successful children's book illustrator and writer, as well as a fine dancer in Merce's company for many years. He was a totally delightful, irreverent, creative, ingenious, dear person. He had no money in those early days, but what he did have was a huge overcoat with capacious pockets. He kept himself and his impoverished friends adequately fed by sliding food into those pockets, as he roamed the various food stores. He also figured out how to dial a number on a public telephone that would allow him to make free calls, and he used a slug (a fake coin) in the subway turnstiles to get inside. Thus he managed life in New York City with panache, if not complete integrity. He was never caught, which I'm sure was due to his charming manner, as well as the fact that his brash actions were based on need rather than cupidity.

Remy Charlip, a beloved Cunningham fellow-dancer between 1950 and 1961. He was also a visual artist, writer,
choreographer, theatre director and designer, and teacher. Here he is in 1954, standing in front of the *Minutiae* set
by Robert Rauschenberg. Courtesy of the Remy Charlip
Estate. Photographer unknown.

Another new student was Sudie Bond, a red-haired off-Broadway
actress. In one class, Sudie brought activity to a halt by dislocating
her shoulder. All of us ("all" added up to perhaps four or five at the
time), including Merce, got into a taxi and accompanied her to the
Emergency Room of the nearest hospital, where she had her shoulder relocated and bound. That ended class for the evening. We were
a tight little community by then.

During that year, 1949–1950, two young women whom I had known in Paris came to New York and joined Merce's class. I have already mentioned Rachel Rosenthal, who had been my classmate and close friend at ÉPJD and who had both a Russian and French background. Tchouky, a young Frenchwoman who had been a model for my artist friends in Paris, also paid a visit to New York, appearing in Merce's studio along with a bottle of Châteauneuf-du-Pape (a very expensive French wine) for her first class. Tchouky returned to Paris after a few months; Rachel stayed. Rachel later became a very successful creative avant-garde actress, director, and drama teacher in Los Angeles. Until her death at age eighty-eight in 2015, her Extreme Theatre Ensemble was called *Tohubohu*. A young Frenchman from the Paris class, François Canton, also joined Merce's class.

# 13

-:-:-:-:-:-:-:-:-:-:-:-:-:-

# EARLIER CUNNINGHAM DANCERS

When I started taking classes with Merce, he had several accomplished dancers with whom he performed at different times and in different dances. Several of them danced in Merce's *A Diversion* and *Games,* on the same program during which we newcomers performed our delightful *Rag-Time Parade,* described further on. I had also seen them dance with Merce on previous occasions. The four, as I remember seeing them dance with him, were Anneliese Widman, Joan Skinner, Dorothy Berea, and Mili Churchill. Joan and Dorothy were members of the Martha Graham Company. I don't know about Anneliese or Mili. They were very different from each other, physically and temperamentally. Anneliese was sturdy, strong, and energetic. Joan filled the kind of roles that later were filled by Carolyn Brown; she was Merce's partner in his lovely duets and was an elegant dancer. Dorothy was muscular, fast, and agile. Mili, whose picture is not as clear in my mind, had, I believe, a more delicate physique and manner. All four performed his dances skillfully but had received dance training from other dancers, so he was not able to start them from zero, as he did with us. Because of previous influences, they carried some mannerisms and habits of movement that were not pure Cunningham. This was the reason he wanted to train his own dancers from the beginning, and we were happy to be his first original products.

None of the four women were in Merce's class in that first year. But as we gained experience and the classes became more advanced, more dancers joined us. I remember being very impressed with Anneliese and Joan, who were far more skilled than we were. I don't have any memory of Dorothy or Mili in class.

I also vividly remember the arrival in class of a very strong, handsome young student named Paul Taylor, and his tall, gorgeous girlfriend Anita Dencks. Paul was a commanding dancer right from the start. He was confident and intensely present. It was inevitable that he would become a company member, and he did. But he was impatient to be a soloist and a lead dancer, so he left after a brief time in Merce's company to build his own company, which is very popular to this day. Anita danced with Merce's company for a number of years, often alternating roles with Viola Farber.

# 14

-:-:-:-:-:-:-:-:-:-:-:-:-:-:-:-

## PASSIONATE DUETS

Merce upset many applecarts in the dance canon, as his choreography developed over sixty years. In the first decade of that development he received largely puzzled looks from whatever public attended performances, and mostly derogatory reviews on those few occasions when a critic deigned to review his performance. The exception to this lack of acceptance occurred during our West Coast tour in 1955, a rare month of enthusiasm from a totally new audience. But it took a good ten years for the dance public to relinquish its expectations of the familiar and develop an appetite for the dances produced by a remarkable and completely novel choreographer. Fortunately, the transition happened.

One applecart Merce did not seek to overturn was the convention of male-female duets, in which the man was the tender and devoted supporter of the woman. There were certainly duets between men or between women, but these never matched in intensity his exquisite male-female duets. Certainly the most obvious difference between mixed-gender duets and same-gender duets is the difference between the male body and the female body, both physically and qualitatively. Since Merce was very tuned in to the way his dancers moved, and choreographed accordingly, this sensitivity of his would be a primary motivating force in the kind of movements he would choose for mixed-gender duets, compared to same-gender duets. It is my belief that this was a prime reason for his choice in partnering.

But perhaps not the only one.

It is hard for me to imagine that Merce would allow himself to be pressured by custom into creating male-female duets. He gave no indication that convention ever occupied space in his imagination; on the contrary, it seemed to provide a stimulus for invention. So there must be an additional motivation that impelled him to carry on what we think of as a tradition.

The fact that Merce was gay in no way prevented him from feeling warm and affectionate toward women, making strong connections with us, and often loving us in his own particular fashion. It would not require a stretch of the imagination to assume that he could enjoy creating such brilliantly intimate and tender duets between a man and a woman. Perhaps this was a means of bringing a part of his fantasy life into being; who can ever know? He was a complex and mysterious human being who expressed everything in his choreography, maybe even parts of himself that never appeared anywhere else.

# 15

-:-:-:-:-:-:-:-:-:-:-:-:-:-

## OUR FIRST PERFORMANCE

In November 1950, Merce was invited to give a lecture/demonstration at the Cooper Union art school in New York City. He would present two of his beautiful solos; two small group pieces with Dorothy Berea, Anneliese Widman, and Mili Churchill; and a hilarious dance called *Ragtime Parade*, to music by Erik Satie. This dance was to be performed by us, his six beginning students, referred to as "the kids." We now had about a year of classes behind us. Our costumes were put together under the outrageous eye of Remy, from odds and ends that we merrily picked out from the endless supply of Second Avenue thrift shops. My costume was a black fishnet flapper dress worn over a crimson silk two-piece bathing suit.

One night, after learning a new step for the dance, Remy and I walked to the subway together. He descended to the downtown platform and I to the uptown platform. Since it was fairly late in the evening, the platforms were empty except for us. So we began rehearsing our new steps on opposite platforms, singing the music and giggling our heads off, until the subway cars arrived and whisked us away from each other.

After lots of rehearsal, the Great Night arrived. We six inexperienced dancers were all very excited and totally primed for the performance. Everything proceeded very well, as we awaited our turn (*Ragtime Parade* was last on the program). The audience was warm and responsive to Merce's beautiful dances, which preceded ours. (Cooper Union was in Greenwich Village, where an audience was always receptive to tradition-breaking events.) After our performance, the audience could not stop clapping and cheering until finally Merce decided we needed to do it again!! We were so proud that we, the beginners, "the kids," as John Cage called us, had been asked to give the evening's only encore.

# PART II

-:-:-:-:-:-:-:-:-:-:-:-:-:-

# PURE CUNNINGHAM

# 16

-:-:-:-:-:-:-:-:-:-:-:-:-:-:-

## ZEN AND THE ART OF MUSIC

Merce's partner, John Cage, was breaking new ground in music in the forties and fifties. Although he was in Paris with Merce in the spring of 1949, I don't remember meeting him or being aware of him. I became familiar with him gradually over the next year. He was easy-going, full of laughter, friendly, cheery, and fun to be around—a steady, comforting spirit who grounded Merce's mercurial nature. (In the book, *Trickster Makes This World*, by Lewis Hyde,[1] John Cage is included as a modern trickster, in his role as a composer who was using chance procedures as a means of eliminating desire from his art.) He was passionately interested in Zen, and struggled to live according to its principles. At times he would teach us about Zen philosophy through stories. One story I remember:

A man arrives in America from Eastern Europe with no money and few skills. He works very hard for many years, living very frugally, saving every penny he can in order to bring his family over. He finally has enough money to buy tickets to bring them to America. He goes out on the dock to purchase the tickets and sees a lively game of poker going on. He sits down, joins the game, and loses every bit of money that he had earned with such effort.

Easy come, easy go.

A lesson in Zen unattachment.


It seems to me that, although unattachment was a difficult goal for John to achieve in daily living, it was possible for him to achieve it through musical composition. John was brilliantly able to detach from Western musical tradition, succeeding in its ultimate rejection in 1952 in his extraordinary silent piano composition, 4'33", performed by David Tudor. It consisted of opening the piano, sitting quietly with a stop watch, closing the piano lid to indicate the end of a "movement," opening it again to begin the next movement, and then closing it after four minutes and thirty-three seconds to indicate the end. The audience exhibited outrage, bewilderment, and fascination. They were decidedly not unattached. For John, the experience showed that ambient sounds were as much music as the piano sounds: a further lesson in unattachment.

By 1951, John had already recorded music for prepared piano, a piano that had all kinds of clips attached to its strings, significantly altering the piano's familiar sound. I found the prepared piano sounds very appealing and new. Another excursion into an untouched world of sound/music, as well as chance procedures, was his *Piece for Twelve Radios*. To "play" these radios, he commandeered various friends, as well as students of Merce's, including me and my older brother Paul. In May of 1951, we performed the composition at the McMillan theater at Columbia University. John's piece, which he conducted with a stop watch, if I remember correctly, was part of a long program of new music, and as a result, we didn't get on stage until close to midnight, an hour when there was not much

*Left to right:* John Cage, me, Earle Brown, all dressed for a party, December 1953. Earle was doubly connected to the Cunningham company: composer of several of its scores and married to dancer Carolyn Brown. Though we all knew John as a composer, musician, colleague, and integral member of company life, I never realized during the 1950s that he and Merce were a couple in private life. Photograph: Marion Rice.

of anything on the radio. There were two of us on each radio, one to read the score (he'd written out a score for each radio) and the other to turn the knob to the requested "station," though many of the numbers on the score, being random, were not stations at all. So there were squeaks and whistles, soft static, occasional bursts of speech, and very occasional bits of music, even a fragment of Mozart. (I recently learned, via the great physicist, Stephen Hawking, that the faint sounds that could be heard between official stations were the sounds of the Big Bang, the beginning of the Universe, which radio waves carried.) There were also silences (except for the faint sounds of the Big Bang), lots of them, since many stations were off the air by that time of night. Not being a complete convert to chance and randomness yet, I cheated a bit, and looked for human sounds despite the score. My brother didn't mind, and nobody else noticed.

# 17

-:-:-:-:-:-:-:-:-:-:-:-:-:-:-:-

# CHANCE REPLACES CHOICE

When I fiddled with the radio dials in an effort to find music or voices, I was improvising. Chance procedures, however, are quite different from improvisation. John and Merce became very engrossed in using chance procedures as a creative force. For his choreography, Merce would make a chart of many kinds of movements: of the head, the arms, the body, the legs. Then he might throw dice, or use the I Ching, to determine which movements were to go together and which movements would follow each other. If one position was on the floor, and the succeeding one was leaping in the air, he would have to create a sequence that would facilitate the transition. This novel procedure was a means of bypassing the limits of the human imagination and the limits of habit and familiarity. (Improvisation cannot do that; it comes from the imagination.) The result was, and is, choreography that is full of surprises, freshness, originality. Chance procedures are used by the composer or choreographer in arranging sounds or movements, but the performers are bound by the results. They do what they are taught, in as precise, full, rhythmically accurate a manner as possible. (In some of Cage's pieces, performers are given moments of improvisation, but never in Cunningham's dances, at least as long as I was in the company.) That was very clear to us when we performed dances that Merce had composed by chance procedures (as well as the early dances not using chance). What we dancers contributed was our unique bodies, spirits, and understanding.

Merce was always very interested in what each dancer brought to his choreography, just because of who we were and how we moved. He usually choreographed parts for us based on what he observed as our individual styles and strengths, always, of course, pushing our boundaries so that we became stronger dancers. This was possible for a small and fairly constant company. It must have become much more difficult later, as the company grew in size and turnover.

Quoting myself from the Dance Critics Panel of June 16, 1984:

> Although everybody . . . talked about his dances as being abstract and dehumanized . . . they were extraordinarily personal because they had to do with who the dancers in the company were, how they moved, what their quality of movement was.

# 18

-:-:-:-:-:-:-:-:-:-:-:-:-

## GLOOMY WEATHER

In those early days, Merce was very moody. In retrospect, his moodiness was not surprising, although I believe most of us didn't understand it. During his previous years dancing in the Martha Graham
Company, he had been recognized by audiences and occasionally
by dance critics as a remarkable and unique dancer; also the company had yearly week-long performances in New York and summer
stints at various colleges, so he was performing with some regularity. Merce left Graham's company in 1946 because he no longer felt
comfortable with her dramatic style of dance and choreography.
Her work was full of storytelling and psychological meaning. He
was developing his own approach to dancing, which would become
increasingly different from Martha's. But the fallout from going out
on his own, unfortunately, was much less opportunity to perform
and much less recognition by the critics and the public. No wonder
he would fall into dark moods.

All the dancers could tell when he was feeling down, heavy, un-communicative, and it made us uneasy. Since I was the daughter of a psychologist and had learned a good bit about human behavior, I felt it my mission, on occasion, to approach him and connect with him in some way. I thought of it as "cheering him up." I would cross his forbidding boundary and chat with him for a few minutes. It was the most loving response I could think of, and he seemed to understand that.

In a journal entry for November 10, 1957, I noted: "Merce's first sadness [of that fall]. Attempted to comfort him." Another, less compassionate, journal entry for January 27, 1958, noted: "Merce back to self-hatred and mild moods. I choose to ignore it."

I wonder now whether Merce's self-hatred was in some part a result of internalizing society's disapproval of and discomfort with gay people and gay relationships. That aspect of his life had to be hidden from the public, which might have felt uncomfortable to him, although he was always a very private person. Certainly New York had its share of gay people, but this was a time well before the gay rights movement, so such relationships were often concealed. Probably more of his self-hatred resulted from his failure to achieve recognition and acceptance of his ground-breaking choreography—approval that he needed and deserved.

# 19

-:-:-:-:-:-:-:-:-:-:-:-:-:-

## FANTASIES MEET REALITY

Many of us dancers were somewhat in love with him, myself included, having little comprehension of homosexuality; neither were many of us aware of his romantic relationship with John Cage. (I didn't become aware of their intimate partnership until after leaving the company, when gay relationships became comfortably public.) There was a whispered story about a woman he'd been in love with, back in Washington state, an affair that had ended unhappily, which explained to us his lack of romantic interest in women. We, his female dancers, could always hope that we might rekindle that interest in ourselves.

In 1953, Merce had a six-week teaching stint at Black Mountain College in North Carolina. He was offered the opportunity to bring dancers of his choosing for the last three weeks, during which he would choreograph dances, culminating in a performance at the end of the summer. The dancers he brought were Carolyn Brown,

JoAnn Melsher, and me. Remy Charlip arrived from Colorado, and Paul Taylor, Viola Farber, and Anita Dencks were already there as students. (On the twenty-two-hour bus trip, on three different buses, from New York to Asheville, North Carolina, I was so stiff from sitting so long, that at one point I tried sitting backward, with my tummy facing the back of the seat. It didn't work.)

Also at Black Mountain were philosopher/artist/writer Mary Caroline (M.C.) Richards and her partner-to-be, the fabulously gifted pianist David Tudor, both close friends of Merce and John.

M.C. was a brilliant multifaceted woman. She was an educator, a poet and writer, and a potter, as well as a delightful friend. Her most famous book was *Centering in Pottery, Poetry, and the Person*.[1] She taught English at Black Mountain College from 1945 to 1951, seminal years in which she met Merce and John and David. She taught at many universities during her eighty-three creative years and lived in several intentional communities.

David Tudor was known as one of the leading performers of avant-garde piano music. He was celebrated for his performances in both Europe and America. He went on to compose electronic music and employ electrical instrument building as a form of composition, often for Merce's dances. Upon Cage's death, he took over as music director of the Merce Cunningham Dance Company.

M.C. decided that I should be Merce's wife, because of my upbeat personality, which would be good for him. We had a great time plotting our approach to this fantasied outcome, which, of course, proceeded nowhere. What did unfold, however, was that my "upbeat personality" alienated Viola Farber. This information was whispered to me—probably by Remy. I don't recall being particularly bothered by it. Viola tended toward moodiness, much like Merce. She and I were never close in the way that Remy, Carolyn, and I were.

Our matrimonial plot reached its zenith on the occasion, that winter, of David Tudor's birthday party. It was held, after one of our performances at the Theatre de Lys (to be discussed further on), in Merce's Greenwich Village dance studio at Sheridan Square, the nicest studio so far. M.C. really encouraged me to try to seduce Merce, so at one point in the evening I climbed on his lap and flirted outrageously. Merce laughed a lot, enjoyed the assault thoroughly, but was most certainly not seduced!

I imagine—now—that, had he reciprocated my romantic longings, I would have been totally nonplussed and confused. These were fantasies of mine that were enjoyable but had no foothold in reality. Actualizing them might have been thrilling but also totally disorienting. At any rate, I was not experienced or mature enough to handle such an outcome.

A further use of my tendency to think like a psychologist emerged in my close friendship with Carolyn. We were quite a pair. I was a Jewish girl from Brooklyn, raised by a freewheeling, progressive mother and a fairly indulgent father. She was a Protestant New Englander, from a somewhat more traditional family. As part of that tradition, Carolyn held Merce to a high standard of behavior, just as she did for herself. She could be disappointed and bewildered if he didn't live up to those standards. He, on the other hand, had a quicksilver temperament, his moods responding to all kinds of stimuli; as I mentioned earlier, he was enormously frustrated at being unnoticed and unappreciated by the larger dance audience and the major critics. There were primarily two reasons for the lack of popular enthusiasm: his choreography had burst out of the conventions audiences were accustomed to; that is, drama and storytelling. Furthermore, his musical/sound accompaniment was strange, unfamiliar, and often unpleasant, especially to the ears of audiences raised on classical scores. His audiences had just recently been able to accept the novelties of Stravinsky. Now they were confronted with the even more contemporary complexities of Cage and his cohort.

When Carolyn would be upset by something Merce had done, including his occasional outbursts of antic high spirits, I would do my best to remind her that he was, after all, a human being, and not the godlike being we liked to project onto him. In her book about Merce and John, *Chance and Circumstance*,[2] Carolyn generously wrote that I "gently taught [her] to grow up."

# 20

-:-:-:-:-:-:-:-:-:-:-:-:-

# THE QUIET YEARS

In the two years between our performance at Cooper Union in 1951 and our summer at Black Mountain in 1953, there had been almost no performances that included the beginning dancers. I had gone on taking regular classes with Merce, as well as ballet classes at the Met. I attended several of Merce's dance concerts at the Hunter Playhouse in New York City, deeply appreciating his marvelous dancing and his unique choreography. I was generally open-minded in regard to the music he used, as my brother Paul and I had been listening to very modern music in our late teens, so all that strangeness just struck me as very adventuresome.

In June of 1952, we neophytes, JoAnn, Remy, Ben Garber, and I, performed at Brandeis University in Waltham, Massachusetts, along with Merce and more experienced dancers: Natanya Neumann, Anneliese Widman, Ronne Aul, Joan Skinner, and Donald McKayle (Natanya and Joan were Martha Graham dancers). The event was called a Festival of the Creative Arts and lasted four days.

We performed in two dances, *Symphonie pour un homme seul*, with musique concrète by Pierre Schaeffer, and *Les Noces*, with music by Igor Stravinsky. *Symphonie* was lots of fun to perform and not too difficult. We mimed various daily activities, like washing hands, to all kinds of weird sounds. In *Les Noces*, we beginners were like a chorus, and had exciting movements like being lifted in the air by our partners. Then, as well as many happy times later, my partner was Remy.

The Brandeis performance was the last time that Merce used dancers who had already been trained by other teachers. By this time, he felt we had sufficient skill to execute his new dances as he wanted them danced: not with the mannerisms and styles of other choreographers, but with the precision and clarity of his particular work.

In the winter of 1953, we gave a studio performance of *Suite by Chance*, in preparation for a March performance of it at the University of Illinois. This very difficult dance was choreographed by chance procedures and was accompanied by music for magnetic tape by Christian Wolff, tape that had been cut up and rearranged by chance. It took us many months to learn the dance, and then many rehearsals to be able to begin to perform it with some accuracy. At the last minute, I was unable to go to the University of Illinois because I'd come down with double staph pneumonia. What a huge disappointment that was for me—and it required a sudden adjustment for the company. As for the pneumonia, it was cured quite rapidly by way of injections of aureomycin and penicillin, recently discovered and used during the carnage of WWII, as a welcome means of enabling many servicemen to survive their injuries. My doctor was astonished and delighted by the speed of my recovery. I believe it was the first time he'd used those antibiotics.

# 21

-:-:-:-:-:-:-:-:-:-:-:-:-

# LAUNCHED

The 1953 summer at Black Mountain is officially considered the beginning of the Merce Cunningham Dance Company. I never thought of it that way, since some of us had performed with Merce several times before, and he had choreographed new work specifically for us. I already felt as if we were his company. At Black Mountain, Merce choreographed and taught us three dances—*Banjo, Septet, Dime-a-Dance*—in the three weeks we were there. He also taught classes and rehearsed his ground-breaking dance, *Suite by Chance.*

The three new dances were all composed to piano music: *Banjo,* to music by Louis Moreau Gottschalk, a New Orleans-born composer and pianist, *Septet* to *Trois Morceaux en forme de poire,* music by the French composer Erik Satie, and *Dime-a-Dance* to nineteenth-century pieces selected by David Tudor from *Music the Whole World Loves.* In these three dances, our movements generally followed the rhythm of the music. That was never to happen

My 1953 drawings of the founding members of the Merce Cunningham
Dance Company at Black Mountain College:

Paul Taylor.

Carolyn Brown.

Remy Charlip.

Viola Farber.

John Cage.

Merce Cunningham.

JoAnn Melsher.

again. *Dime-a-Dance* was only performed a few more times; *Banjo* remained in the repertoire for several more years. Only *Septet* has lasted for many years, both as a staple of the Cunningham company and by being taught to other dance companies.

Film clips of a 1955 performance of *Banjo* have survived in the Jacob's Pillow Dance Archive and have even been viewable online in recent years. This piece was a delight to perform: for one reason, we women were thrilled to wear dresses instead of the usual leotards and tights. In addition, it was a lively, joyous romp all the way through, and our interactions with each other were full of eye contact and smiles.

*Septet* was a lovely dance, divided into seven sections with very different dynamics: among them, dreamy, amorous, playful, solemn, sad. (Vivid fragments of a 1955 performance, with me dancing, are also in the Pillow Archive; I was happily surprised to see them in 2015.) There was a great deal of stillness in it: in fact, the opening of the dance appeared to display three female statues, which then came to life as a very fluid Merce danced around them. The combinations of dancers varied—solo, duet, trio, quartet, group; there were times of individual movements and times of simultaneous, coordinated ones. It was easy to read stories of love and separation into *Septet*, even before we learned of the titles Merce gave to the sections: In the Garden, In the Music Hall, In the Tea House, In the Playground, In the Morgue, In the Distance, In the End. The Erik Satie score, *Trois Morceaux en forme de poire* (*Three Pieces in the Form of a Pear*—a tongue-in-cheek title created by Satie in response to criticisms of "lack of form" in his compositions) was exquisite, almost hypnotic at moments.

*Dime-a-Dance* consisted of thirteen short dances, varied in tempo, each very appealing. Which dances were performed, and in what order was determined by chance. By paying a dime, an audience member could pick one card from a deck of thirteen playing cards, each card representing a specific dance that was to be performed. *Dime-a-Dance* survived in the repertory for only two more

Photograph from the 1953 Black Mountain College season. *Left to right:* Viola Farber, Merce, Carolyn Brown, Paul Taylor.

performances, but it was very enjoyable to dance. One of its sections did appear many years later in a Cunningham Event.

An Event, which was only developed after my time in the company, is a site-specific performance. It comprises selections from different full-length dances, unified seamlessly into a new dance and accompanied by newly chosen music. Over time, Events have varied in length, from ninety minutes to thirty minutes. Its format was invented by Merce to facilitate performing in a nontheatrical space. The first Event was created for a performance in a museum in Vienna, Austria, June 1964. In the twentieth century, Events were one-time-only occurrences: if you went to the next evening's performance in the same space, you found the dances or the casting had changed—or, often, both. During the twenty-first century, the same dancers often performed the same material in several Events, but often with the dances occurring simultaneously on two or more stages, as they did during the company's final performances at the Park Avenue Armory, December 29–31, 2011. "My mind always inclines toward complexity," Merce liked to say with a twinkle.

Both *Banjo* and *Septet* made it easy for audiences to relax, enjoy, and respond with enthusiasm. Audiences could delight in the musical accompaniment and its relationship to the movement, and in *Septet* they, like us, could relate to the mood of the different sections and make up stories. This was a rare respite for audiences that Merce was already challenging with his innovative choreography, his use of chance procedures, and his disconnection of dance from music. (The music and the dance were composed separately and only came together when each was completed.) He was also using musical accompaniment that for many people was strange and often unpleasant.

One of the revelations of our rehearsals was hearing David Tudor play Louis Moreau Gottschalk's *Banjo*. It's an incredibly dense, complex, lively piece of piano music requiring an extremely skillful pianist. David played it brilliantly and with ease. He was equally masterful in his execution of *Septet*, a piece for four hands, which he played gorgeously with just two. (The other revelation at Black Mountain was the discovery of yogurt and blackstrap molasses, served at every meal. I'd never known of either food before and have been grateful ever since, at least for the yogurt. I can do without the molasses.)

For the second, and fortunately last time in my dance career, I was unable to dance at the culminating performance. This time, after wonderful intense rehearsals, two days before the performance I badly sprained my ankle. (Recent X-rays have indicated that I actually fractured it. X-rays in the fifties didn't show the fracture.) I was always so thrilled when, in a section of a dance, I was partnered with Merce. At the moment of the fracture, I was doing a wonderful

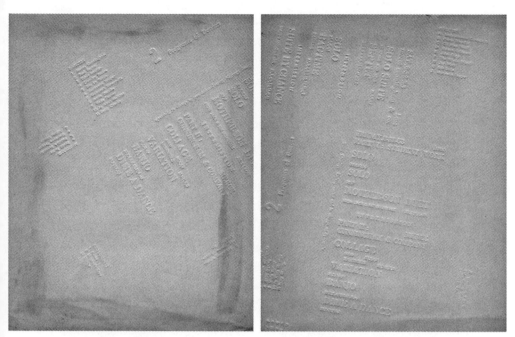

This embossed Black Mountain program, very hard to read, was designed by Remy Charlip.

section of *Dime-a-Dance* where I leaped high in the air along with Merce. Unfortunately, my enthusiasm crashed, along with me, as I landed on the side of my foot instead of the sole. Everyone was stunned. I was taken to the nearest hospital, where they X-rayed my ankle. On my return, Merce hastily divided my parts in the dances among two aspiring students and future company members, Viola Farber and Anita Dencks, and simply left out sections that couldn't be taught in such a short time. It was a devastating blow, but we all pulled together and managed to offer a fine concert.

Happily, I was still able to perform the guitar music I'd composed for Paul Taylor's choreography, presented on the same program. The Black Mountain College community was wildly enthusiastic about everything.

*Dime-a-Dance* was particularly fun for me. I had studied mime when I was in Paris at the drama school, ÉPJD. Marcel Marceau, the great French mime, was our teacher for the first few weeks I was there. Then he became too busy performing, and another excellent teacher, who I believe was Roger Desmare, a member of his company, replaced him. Merce assigned me a miming introduction to the dance. I would walk to the front of the stage, mime winding up an old phonograph machine, open the lid, pull out a record from the cabinet below, put it on the turntable, place the armature with the needle onto the record, and the music would start. (I had actually physically performed those actions with our phonograph when I was a little girl, so it was familiar.) Fortunately, we performed the piece a few times after Black Mountain, so I had the satisfaction of doing that introduction, as well as successfully leaping in my duet with Merce.

We returned home from Black Mountain, after our great success. John Cage, who acted as manager for the company as well as composer, mother, comforter, and whatever else was needed, snared us an entire week of performances (unheard of for a modern dance company) at the Theatre de Lys in Greenwich Village. It was set for vacation week, the end of December. The Theatre de Lys was a tiny theater with a tiny stage, hardly the best showcase for such lively and expansive dances, but we were thrilled and determined to stun the unsuspecting New York audience. We performed the same dances as we had at Black Mountain, while Merce added several solos of his own.

The house was full for each performance—always attended by many artists from the Abstract Expressionist school, such as Robert Motherwell, Lee Krasner, Franz Kline, Willem de Kooning, Philip Guston, as well as young upstart artists like Ray Johnson, all of whom adored Merce's choreography. We managed well in the limited stage space, which had been expanded for our performances. Many of our friends and families attended the concerts and gave us support and appreciation.

The last dance on the program was *Suite by Chance*, which was both difficult and physically draining. The only part of the dance

Photographs from around the time of the 1953 Cunningham season at the Theatre de Lys, New York:

*Above left:* Offstage with Merce. Photograph: George Moffett.

*Above right:* Rehearsing with Merce. Our hands, heads, and proximity all make this special to me. Photographer unknown.

*Left:* Camaderie offstage. Me (with Remy Charlip's head behind); Merce; Carolyn Brown. Date uncertain. Photo: George Moffett.

Merce's *Banjo* (1953). *Left to right:* Timothy LaFarge and JoAnn Melsher; Remy Charlip and me; Carolyn Brown, Merce, and Anita Dencks. Photo by Arnold Eagle. We adored to dance this extrovert piece, a section of which has survived on a 1955 silent film taken at Jacob's Pillow.

Me in Merce's *Fragments*. We, the Cunningham company, danced the premiere of this in its Theatre de Lys season in New York in December 1953. As so often in Merce's choreography, my body is facing in multiple directions at the same time. Photographer unknown.

that I remember was right near the end, when we had to do a series of pirouettes. By then, I was worn out and could barely keep myself centered. A former boyfriend of mine came backstage after the performance and commented acidly, "You looked exhausted by the end of that last dance." I was very cross after that interchange, and Carolyn said it was the only time she'd ever seen me cranky.

As I mentioned above, after one of the performances the company, as well as associated friends, celebrated David Tudor's birthday at Merce's studio. M.C. Richards enacted the three roles of a very short, absurdist Gertrude Stein play, *In a Garden*, to much applause and delight. I had prepared a speech for David in French, which began with the statement, "Il n'y a que le temps et l'espace" (There is only time and space), and proceeded impudently with a comical version of John Cage's philosophy. It concluded with a sly innuendo: "Moi, j'ai le temps; as-tu l'espace?" (I have the time; have

A New York newspaper advertisement for the Cunningham company's December 1953 season at the Theatre de Lys, New York.

you the space?) accompanied by batting eyelashes and an irresistible smirk. Everyone loved it. Unfortunately, I don't have the rest of the speech either in writing or in my memory.

I'm not sure whether it was at this party or at another that John and David, serious students of Zen Buddhism, performed the Japanese Tea Ceremony, with great deliberateness, care, and exquisite perfection. It was fascinating to watch such an unfamiliar ritual from a very different culture.

## 22

-:-:-:-:-:-:-:-:-:-:-:-:-

# IN ADDITION TO DANCING

Many years later, when I would visit Merce after a performance, he would regale me with stories about me. One of these took place in those early years of teaching, when he had a handful of students, all of whom were barely getting by financially: "You collected the class fees from each student," he recalled, "and gave it to me, because I could never ask for payment. I asked you how you could stand asking for money from them. You told me, 'I put out my hand and turn my face away,' in order to avoid seeing their struggle."

Another story Merce loved to tell was about my efforts, in the early days of classes, to "understand" the movement sequences he would give us. After one particularly difficult exercise in class, I asked him, in great frustration, "How can I possibly do that!?" His wise response: "Marianne, the only way to do it is to do it." My first experience with a koan.

During this period of time I earned my B.A. degree in French at New York University, taught dance in Woodmere, Long Island, then at Rye Country Day School, a private elementary school in Westchester County, and finally spent five years teaching dance, drama, and world literature at New Lincoln School on 110th Street in New York City. There I met, and in 1956 married my first husband, Sid Simon, a very creative and influential teacher, later a college professor and author of many books on Values Clarification and other aspects of education. Merce and John came to our wedding reception, which was held in a large loft on Second Avenue that belonged to friends of ours. As a wedding gift, Merce and John gave us an enormous Le Creuset red-enameled casserole pot, which I still regularly use and, of course, treasure. They probably spent several months' rent on it. I have a movie of that wedding reception. In one scene, I'm walking around and Merce pops up from behind a chair, grinning, and I give him a shove, laughing.

My remarkably accepting father helped support me so I could continue dancing with the company while working part-time. After all, the only time we were paid as dancers was during our week performing at the Theatre de Lys, a union theater. Merce's concerts were so few and far between at that time that he could barely afford to live, and he certainly could not afford to pay his dancers.

During these years, I lived in a number of apartments; in the East Village, the West Village, and eventually on the Upper East Side. My first one-room apartment on Jane Street cost twenty-five dollars a month. The last apartment on East 69th Street and First Avenue was a cold-water flat (that is, it had hot water but no heat). It cost thirty dollars a month and when they put in heat the rent was raised to forty dollars a month. Life in New York City was remarkably affordable, so all of us managed to get by, with or without being paid as dancers.

In the early fifties, M.C. Richards was translating Antonin Artaud's book, *Le Théâtre et Son Double (The Theatre and Its Double)* from the French language. Since she knew that I had spent a year in Paris and was fairly fluent in French, she asked me to help her translate certain parts of the book with which she was having difficulty.

I was happy to do so. In grateful appreciation, she gave me a typed copy of her manuscript, which I have safely kept. In his text, published in 1938, Artaud was demanding a radical shift in theatrical conventions. (Similarly, Merce and John were creating radical shifts in dance and music.) To quote Artaud in chapter 8, titled "The Theater of Cruelty": "Instead of continuing to rely upon texts which are considered to be final and sacred, it is most important to break the subjugation of theater to text, and to recover the notion of a kind of unique language half-way between gesture and thought." Not an easy request; yet it presaged works by such playwrights as Samuel Beckett and David Mamet, as well as performance artists like Rachel Rosenthal, and The Living Theater in New York; also the Judson Dance Theater in New York. I was personally very comfortable with such ideas.

I attended as many dance performances as I could while studying with Merce: the New York City Ballet, Sadler's Wells Ballet. Among the modern dance companies and individuals I remember seeing were Sybil Shearer, Katherine Litz, José Limón, Hanya Holm, Jean Erdman, Sophie Maslow, Charles Weidman, and Doris Humphrey. There were also a number of ethnic dance performances—Indian, Flamenco, and Japanese Kabuki theater, which was very dance-like. I saw performances by African-American dancers Katherine Dunham and Pearl Primus. The more familiar I became with Merce's choreography, the less interesting I found other modern dancers. I never lost interest in ballet or ethnic dance, however.

Once in a while I would ask my father to take Merce out to dinner with us, because I knew Merce had such a hard time making ends meet. My father would oblige, and Merce would have a splendid big meal to fortify himself for the lean times ahead. It was such a pleasure to be able to give him something, in exchange for all he gave us. And, of course, I was always happy to be in his genial company. Despite the moodiness that might show up in class or rehearsal, in social situations Merce was dependably charming and engaged. At least, that was my experience of him, as well as my father's. I imagine that my father might have felt familiar to Merce, since both his father and mine were professionals in the business world.

In a similar culinary vein, my journal describes a lovely event on January 3, 1958: "Feast for the dance company at our apartment. Merce, John, David, Nick [Cernovitch], Remy, Carolyn, Cynthia [Stone] and us. Very nice! They brought cumquats, Châteauneuf-du-Pape and Schrafft's cookies, and appreciated everything enormously—food, wine, maté, home preserves, movies and slides of dances. They looked at our photograph albums, books, etc. Just so nice and so satisfying to me to have them here and make it all so real and part of life instead of a compartment. They left at 12:30."

One time, in the early 1950s, Rachel Rosenthal's parents had a huge party at their splendid duplex apartment opposite Central Park. Of course, all the Cunningham students were invited, as well as Merce and John, David Tudor and M.C. Richards. Our hosts had an enormous spread of gourmet foods, which for most of the dancers and musicians was an irresistible attraction. John's memorable words: "I've been eating all day so that my stomach would stretch and I could eat a whole lot tonight." Just the opposite of what most people do, to prepare for a delicious and endless gustatory indulgence. There was no conventional approach for John.

Speaking of "no conventional approach," I remember asking John, once, on our first big tour on the West Coast, "What would you do if your music were generally accepted?" His response was, "I'd do something else." Perhaps tongue in cheek, I don't know, but it seemed to fit him so well.

During my years in the company, there were times when I felt very discouraged about my dancing and would find Merce's classes too intimidating. So I would avoid them for a period of time. I'd continue to take ballet classes; then after a while I'd go back to his studio and pitch in again. In a journal entry from January 3, 1958, I wrote: "Rehearsal class—so hard I couldn't do anything—felt like I wasn't dancing or a dancer and working like an athlete. Remy says

Merce's *Minutiae* (1954) had its premiere at the Brooklyn Academy of Music (in its Music Hall): costumes by Remy Charlip, set by Robert Rauschenberg (his first designs for the Cunningham company). Prolonged balance on one leg was always a feature of Merce's choreography, but I lacked feet that could point. *Left to right:* Viola Farber, me, Karen Kanner. Photograph: John G. Ross.

you must attend his classes regularly if at all—then it becomes possible. So I'll stay at ballet until I get further, then do both." But in a journal entry of February 28, just over a month later, I wrote: "Rehearsal with Merce and brilliant class, flying across the floor." Apparently, I made a quick recovery!

The fact is, I lacked some of the finer points of technique—turnout, leg extension, feet that could point (despite the encouraging comment by the Cornell doctor), as the above photo demonstrates. Much of it was the way I was built, and some was because I started dancing so late, compared to many others in the company. I was, however, very strong, and did fine jumps and leaps. Also, there was one movement in the quartet in *Septet* that demonstrated that

Merce's *Septet* (1953). *Left to right:* me, Carolyn, Merce, Viola Farber. Despite my less than ideal feet, I was strong. Merce's choreography here showcased my ability to descend slowly to the floor while keeping my right leg off the floor: "queen of the mountain," as Carolyn Brown wrote to me in 1998.

strength. I was standing upright on my left foot with my right leg and foot extended to the side several inches off the floor. I slowly descended to a squatting position, with my right leg and foot still off the floor, while holding on to Merce's arm. Carolyn has taught *Septet* to many companies and has assured me that no one else has ever done that move while keeping her right foot off the floor. She wrote to me in 1998 that I was "still Queen of the Mountain," a lovely and most welcome validation.

In retrospect, I was fortunate to have been present when the company formed. Had I arrived later, I suspect I might not have been selected for the company, despite my enthusiasm and lively spirit.

# 23

-:-:-:-:-:-:-:-:-:-:-:-:-:-:-:-

# OUR COMPANY MEMBERS
# AND DESIGNERS

Carolyn soon became the lead dancer in the company, usually part-nering with Merce and eventually given solos to perform. She was an exquisite dancer. She was a perfectionist about her dancing, and it served her well. Her technique was excellent and constantly de-veloping. Her movements were pure, clear and precise. She'd been dancing since childhood—her mother taught dance. She learned rapidly and was breathtaking to watch, both in slow and fast move-ments. In my journal entry of February 24, 1958: "Carolyn is re-markable, she does everything so fully and beautifully and well."

Viola was a most interesting dancer. Rather than being lithe and graceful, she had an awkwardness in her movements that Merce and John found utterly fascinating, and that Merce accentuated in his choreography for her. This unique awkwardness is visible in the background of the photograph of Merce and me. In addition, she

Merce's *Suite by Chance* (1952). *Left to right:* Viola Farber, me, Merce. The way a single moment catches three dancers in three different positions is quintessential Cunningham, as is the strength of that outstretched hand of his to support me. Merce and John were fascinated by the quality of compelling awkwardness in Viola's dancing.

was technically very gifted, and was able to do whatever she was given to do. She added a whole other dimension to the company. Furthermore, she was an excellent pianist, and from time to time would play for class. In my journal entry from February 28, 1958, I concluded by writing: "Viola wild on the keyboard." She could also come up with moments of comic brilliance away from the piano. In a journal entry, July 1, 1958: "Viola put on a riotous performance as masseuse on Carolyn's legs and my feet, talking to them as if they were a dog and a cat."

When Remy was dancing in the company, he was in his early twenties but was already bald across the top of his head. For whatever reason, aesthetic or neurotic, who knows, this fact caused Merce and John great consternation. (Actually, in those days, bald dancers did not exist—they all wore toupees or wigs.) Merce and John fussed about it, and Merce, in his typically indirect, round-about manner, managed to have gossip reach Remy's ear, the gossip implying that Remy should wear a toupee. Remy complied for a while, wanting to pacify the aura of criticism, though never aware that the suggestion originally came from Merce. He eventually gave up wearing it, which left Merce and John uncomfortable, but no more was said about it. Remy was a lovely, lively dancer, and he danced in the company for many years. And in the early years, before Bob Rauschenberg and Jasper Johns got involved, Remy's artistry and inventiveness proved invaluable with designs. He would find and put together excellent costumes, and planned programs and publicity, all at minimal cost. Despite all that, I suspect he never felt fully embraced by either Merce or John. All of the other company members adored him, throughout his years as a Cunningham dancer.

Because the dances were about movement, rather than storytelling, almost all of the costumes, with a few exceptions, consisted of tights and leotards, beautifully colored and decorated. Here is a journal entry about costumes, November 11, 1957: "Bob and Jap [Jasper] sprayed it [many colors of paint or dye] right on me [I had on white tights and a white leotard] and I look like a harlequin. It's beautiful." This probably refers to the costume for *Labyrinthian Dances*.

Another journal entry about costumes, November 30, 1957: "I went to the Brooklyn Academy of Music. *Springweather* costumes quite unexpected—bosom cut very low, pink and blue awful offal, elastic bands to sew in *Labyrinthian Dances* costumes. Sewed madly between and after rehearsal. Sewed each other into skirts for *Springweather*."

Bob Rauschenberg had become very interested in Merce's choreography in 1953, having met John and Merce at Black Mountain College two years previously. He soon became the company's set and costume designer, a role that Remy had filled with delightful improvisational ingenuity until then. Remy was now ready to abandon his role as costume and set designer, instead focusing on his dancing with Merce and several other choreographers, his design work for Judith Martin's theatre/dance company, and his upcoming career as a children's book illustrator.

Jasper (Jap) Johns arrived in New York in 1954, after a stint in the army during the Korean War. He met Bob and they soon became partners in life and work, occupying lofts, one above the other, in a building in lower Manhattan that also briefly housed Rachel Rosenthal. Buildings that had been home to small manufacturing businesses were now available as inexpensive studios and, sometimes illegally, living quarters. To earn an income, Bob and Jasper designed elegant display windows for large, uptown and upscale department stores.

Bob was warm, friendly, and easy-going, unfazed by last-minute challenges to his set designs, and delighted to improvise new ones within a very short turnaround time. Here is an example, quoting from Carolyn Brown's *Chance and Circumstance*: "[Just before a performance at the Brooklyn Academy of Music:] The fire inspectors took one look at the original *Nocturnes* set, declared it unsafe, and banned its use. . . . Bob relished a challenge. . . . After a brief consultation, he and Jap disappeared. . . . They returned an hour or so later carrying carton-loads of artificial greenery, all certifiably fire-resistant, and within minutes they'd dismantled the old set and created a new one. . . . Rauschenberg: the mischievous, merry-making, ever-resourceful wizard!"

Bob created a delightful set for *Minutiae*, choreographed in 1954. The set consisted of three standing screens, heavily textured, colored bold orange. (A version of this set was later to become a component of many Cunningham Events, and has appeared in several exhibitions featuring Cunningham and/or Rauschenberg.) We interacted with the screens throughout the dance, going behind them and emerging from them. At the beginning of the dance, I sat behind one of the screens, reading the comics which happened to be

Merce's *Minutiae* (1954) at the Brooklyn Academy of Music, with Remy Charlip costumes and Robert Rauschenberg set. Photographs: John G. Ross.

*Left to right*: Viola Farber and Merce; Karen Kanner (kneeling); Carolyn Brown, Remy Charlip (lying on floor, wearing toupee), me.

*Left to right*: me (on floor), Viola Farber, Carolyn Brown, Karen Kanner.

*Left:* (*Left to right*) Carolyn Brown, me, Karen Kanner, costumed by Remy Charlip, before the set by Robert Rauschenberg.

*Below:* Carolyn (*left*) and me, long-term friends onstage and offstage.

glued right in front of me. I then became visible on stage by sliding out around the screen. I loved that entrance. Merce once said about *Minutiae* that he composed it after looking out the studio window and watching people walking in the street. He later recanted and said he'd just made that story up.

Jasper, unlike Bob, was more serious, introverted, private. In fact, their artwork differed in the same way as their personalities: Jasper's more thoughtful, intellectual; Bob's more improvisational, even mischievous. Since my personality had more in common with Bob's than with Jasper's, I immediately responded emotionally and physically to Bob's artwork, and have continued to do so over the years. I admire Jasper's work but don't have that immediate visceral response to it.

I was always interested in what was new in the art world and would frequently ramble through the art galleries lining 57th Street, with curiosity and relish. I particularly enjoyed the Abstract Expressionist artists' work, its vigor and variety, but also the newer styles that were appearing. These included Bob's and Jasper's work as well as the work of other artists whom Merce selected as set designers in later years, such as Roy Lichtenstein and Andy Warhol. In the late sixties, Warhol, interested in the intersection of art and science, exhibited silver mylar balloons, inflated with helium. They were like silver clouds. Merce saw the exhibit and worked with Warhol to use the balloons as part of the set for his new dance, *RainForest*. As dancers moved, the untethered "silver clouds" bounced around the stage—they were at different heights from the floor, and easily bumped into or affected by nearby movement. I found that delightful and startling to watch.

# 24

-:-:-:-:-:-:-:-:-:-:-:-:-:-

## JOURNEYING TO PERFORMANCES

Periodically, we would be invited to dance at some college or university. We would all travel together in the Volkswagen microbus—Merce, John, the dancers, David Tudor, Bob Rauschenberg, Nick Cernovitch (lighting), the sets, and costumes. We were a large family. Several of us would take turns driving. We would drive out one day, perform, stay overnight in a dorm or motel, and drive home the next day. I remember John spotting a large puffball (mushroom) in a field (he was becoming a mycologist–mushroom expert) and demanding we stop the car. He got out and harvested the puffball. We stopped at a state park for supper, cooking steak over a fire, along with the puffball, which was delicious. My mother once said, "I don't mind you dancing with those crazy people, but DON'T EAT THOSE MUSHROOMS!!"

Actually, at some point a story went around that confirmed my mother's vigorous caution. John had invited a group of friends to dinner, featuring selected mushrooms elegantly cooked. Later that evening all his guests, including John, got sick. Happily no one died.

In a journal entry for June 29, 1958, I described one of those trips: "We left at 6:15 or so. Gorgeous day. Soft tenderly pink morning, cool, fine light. As we went we saw lovely fields of soft colors—purple flowers, yellow, and all the colors of meadow. We had a picnic lunch next to a stream. David identified purslane, a delicious edible weed. We waded in the stream. I drove for several hours to the Ohio border, talking to Merce.

[I asked:] "'How did your technique evolve?'

[He responded:] "'The human body should be able to do anything. A person must find the point of balance. One must learn what movement is—by moving. I use forty minute warm-ups because during them students get a chance to stretch out, I can control their work, while in the last part of class one concentrates more on learning and rhythm, etc. The knowledge is slowly carried over. The excitement is to see someone learn to dance. I do not support my students all the way—they must work much themselves—but this really develops an independent dancer. Teach them realistically, let them make their own images. Don't get under their skin emotionally and possess them. No need for symbols and mysticism—learn craft. Learn by experience, work it out yourself with a well-placed word or suggestion, keep reality and image separate and let the student join them. Experience center.'"

And part of the same day: "Great splendid cook-out at a park just inside Ohio—steak, corn, yams, salad, wine, strawberries. The grounds emptied out shortly after our arrival. Beautiful evening, barefoot, under great silver beech trees, near a lake. An almost full moon in a shining sky. We were full of laughter and good feeling. Day-lilies by thousands, cornflowers, lavender, pink and white clover, roses. Drove to Cleveland area motel around 12:30."

And the next morning: "Breakfast in diner and off we went. Countryside got flatter and flatter, but so full of color. John stopped for mushrooms in someone's yard. For lunch, another small town allowed us its lake and tree-filled park. Girls swam. Swings. Back in the bus. Merce divulged his knitting was for the summer, a costume with four arms—'like some people look when they are undecided,' he said. It's for himself. [The sweater became his costume for the solo *Antic Meet*.] We finally arrived at 7, New York time, 6 here [Muncie, Indiana]. Dined in town and played game of guessing the person [The person who's 'it' asks questions; the others answer 'yes' or 'no']. Much hilarity."

More experiences of great conversations while traveling by car:

December 16, 1957: "On way to Boston long conversation with David, Nick and John on Anthroposophy, Zen, reincarnation, spiritual research, matter vs. spirit."

December 16, 1957: "All nine of us piled in the VW and drove off to NYC. I talked to Merce lots on the way. Of teaching and dancing. He teaches composition in movement, time and space. Space: person as the center wherever he is on stage (arena style) instead of fitting to the frame and audience. Time: measured in length, not pulse. Movement: still, and some moving. Slow and fast. Merce said, in response to my question, and without even stopping to think, that *Changeling* and *Labyrinthian Dances* were his favorites of all pieces ever done." [Merce had just composed those two dances in 1957.]

And finally, July 3, 1958, a conversation about Zen with John: "'Eastern philosophy—Arrive at openness, tolerance, acceptance, oneness with the world by starting with the world and coming to your tiny place in it. Avoid feeling separate and competitive by eliminating ego and its demands.' But he thought it possible to arrive there via the Western self first. Then he spoke of trying to make his life all one fabric illumined by Zen, rather than compartments. Trying to fit caution and discrimination of mushrooming with unseparateness of Zen. Said he lived in community mostly to learn how to live with people and still be himself, be able to get mad at people when necessary. Talked of situational behavior in this world of many worlds."

# 25

-:-:-:-:-:-:-:-:-:-:-:-:-:-

# BREAKING NEW GROUND

In 1955, Merce choreographed *Springweather and People,* a very long, lyrical dance that I thoroughly enjoyed and that was one of the early ones for which the music was composed completely separately from the dance, and where Merce used a stopwatch. The composer was Earle Brown, Carolyn Brown's husband. He called the score *Indices.* The score was twenty-nine minutes long, the same length as the dance. Earle was one of several contemporary composers whom Merce invited to create music for his dances. He, along with John Cage, Christian Wolff, and Morty Feldman, left behind traditional methods of composition and broke new ground using chance procedures, open-form music, and indeterminacy in performance. All four of them are considered the greatest composers of that period. Earle claimed as his influences Gertrude Stein and James Joyce, as well as Alexander Calder and Jackson Pollock.

*Springweather and People* featured many moments of stillness, stillness as part of movement, as Merce and John have described it.

In fact, at one point in the dance, a group of four of us stood in one place and position for what seemed like fifteen minutes, though it was actually a much shorter time. We weren't doing nothing—we were standing still. It was not a time to relax and rest, but more like a bird stopping in midflight on the tip of a branch, before taking off again. At the time, no such directions were given to us. We were just told to stay in whatever position we were in for a certain number of counts. We were certainly too busy paying attention to the counts and to what was going on around us to relax or rest. Stillness as part of movement was the result, no matter what we were told or not told.

Quoting myself from the Dance Critics Panel, June 16, 1984:

When we first did Springweather, Merce was convinced that there was no way that we could ever get together or figure out where we were at different times. We were just counting and we had nothing to do with the music. [But as rehearsals went on] we did hear [the music] a number of times, and after a while Merce said, "How is it that you keep being together at these different times?" And we said, "Well, we have musical cues." That was because we were so naive that we listened to whatever was presented to us and heard it as music and used it the same way that we would use other music. We would hear a squeak or a beep and we would know that we were supposed to all be in a certain portion of the stage. So Merce was quite surprised by our ingenuity.

Philosophically, there was undoubtedly a Zen connection between Merce's stillness in movement, John's silence in music, and Bob's all-white paintings. As far as I can remember, I didn't make those connections at the time. I was just focused on dancing as well as possible.

When we were in rehearsal for *Springweather*, we made a discovery about the limits of our attention span. It seemed at every rehearsal we would start falling into giggles and goofiness after 10 PM.

It became a kind of cliché for us—we'd start to be silly and someone would immediately say, "It must be 10 o'clock," and sure enough, it was. It would not be surprising if our giddiness had irritated Merce, but he never let it show, if indeed he felt annoyed.

Another of our youthful foibles was making up and sharing little stories about what was happening in the dances, since they were always taught as pure movement. I remember feeling that it was very necessary to have something to hang onto, like a little story, because it was all so new. Those stories were occasionally shared with Merce. He would respond with an enigmatic smile or chuckle. It is likely he had his own stories or images related to his dances, but he didn't share them with, or impose them on his dancers. In fact, I would guess that the stories or images presented themselves to him in the form of movements and sequences of movement, rather than as a drama that would then be translated into or illustrated by a dance. Given his remarkable body that could do anything, it seems likely that he experienced life in its many aspects—emotional, intellectual—primarily through physical movement, which he might then express in his choreography, or translate into verbal or written commentary (he was a very articulate writer and speaker). Just as we describe people as being mainly visual or auditory, Merce was essentially physical. Watching his dances, one can project on them all kinds of narrative and drama. Merce knew his audiences would do that. He didn't mind at all.

# 26

-:-:-:-:-:-:-:-:-:-:-:-:-:-

## OUR FIRST GRAND TOUR

In 1955, John arranged an exciting three-week tour of the West Coast for us—the first extended company tour ever. We were to perform in California, Oregon, and Washington and would be housed mostly by friends of John and Merce. We planned to fly to California, an amazing experience for all of us New York–based dancers. After our performances there, we'd go north by train to our various performance destinations.

Postcard to my parents in New York, November 2, 1955, Hollywood, California: "Arrived—fantastic altogether—the trip and this crazy city—now awaiting train to Santa Barbara."

Santa Barbara was our first major stop. We were housed by our generous hosts, the Morgan family, in a guest cottage with a swimming pool, on top of a mountain overlooking the city. We loved every minute of the five days spent in such luxury, and we had one performance, which was well reviewed, as were all our performances on that tour—quite a shocking change from New York, where none of the dance critics bothered to review our dancing.

Here is a letter to my parents in New York, November 6, 1955, from Santa Barbara:

We are now all lounging on a lawn overlooking a pool overlooking the hills and valley of Santa Barbara, hung over with a white mist which comes about halfway up our mountain range and then stops. We see lots of tree-covered mountains, sagebrush of pale blue and violet, distant flat houses. A soft breeze blows.

In back of us is a splendid low rambling adobe house that melts into the mountain and is the most fabulous house I have ever wanted. Inside are many rooms on all different levels, patios with plants and flowers, a magnificent 3-room bathroom consisting of dressing room, toilet room and a huge bath made of terrazzo set in a room with a gilt wood ceiling and faint gold-painted adobe wall and fieldstone floor. A large French window with tan drapes opens onto a balcony that overlooks mountains and valleys. The toilet room also has this view.

All the fittings in the house are most elegant, gorgeous furniture and paintings and nooks of the kind I adore, lots of beautiful old painted chests, old solid wood tables, etc. You can imagine, since you know my taste. And a bedroom wing with many rooms, also on different levels and with gorgeous mountain views. At night thousands of stars, and lights of Santa Barbara below us.

The hosts are fine genial very generous people with 4 kids—3, 9, 11, 12—who bring friends over and really enjoy the wealth. We are living in a separate guest house with a bedroom with 4 bunk beds, a living room, kitchen, bath, and 2 feet to the pool. The Cunningham Co. living rough, eh?

Performed Friday night. During *Banjo*, I tripped over the wing curtain and hung on it beautifully for several minutes.

Otherwise fine performance in elegant old theatre. Reception in Green Room after, and party here after that. We are being banqueted, feted and generally treated like conquering heroes. All meals supplied plus $5. pin money which we have absolutely no need for.

Another performance destination, arrived at by train, was San Diego, where Carolyn and I had a sweet adventure at the station. Apparently, a very elegant house had been destined to host Merce and John, by the woman who owned it. But her husband, who was the architect of the house, also met the train at the station, and was quite taken by two lovely young women (us), and invited us to their house before his wife could snare Merce! The house was an architectural gem, with a cantilevered roof, on a high hill overlooking a vast plain. It had a sunken conversation pit in the living room. In our bedroom, our beds cranked into sitting positions for breakfast in bed! I'm sure there must have been some heavy couple conversations initiated by that frustrated wife, who had been looking forward to the great honor of hosting Merce and John, rather than two young women.

Letter to my parents, November 13, 1955, from San Diego, California:

Well, each is more fabulous than the last. Carolyn and I stayed 2 nights in the most beautiful pure modern house I have ever seen. The home of an architect and his designer wife. He designed the place—up in mountains—all glass and light wood, white cement floors radiantly heated, beautiful fabrics on the windows and over closets, aluminum chairs with brilliant colored strips on them, many gem-colored pillows around a set-in foam rubber round couch built into the floor with a round metal sort of fireplace in the middle. Such tranquility and peace here.

He was just charming—mind racing off lyrically and imaginatively, very humorous, cheerful, and intelligent in a really liberated way. His wife lovely looking but very managerial and iron. Oh, here, too, the bathroom was marvelous—large, windowed, huge tub, carpeted floor, and you flush the toilet by pressing a penny [that is] lying on the floor.

We performed last night in a H.S. auditorium with an enthusiastic audience and did the best overall performing to date—because everyone was so nice to us—they were sort of involved in a crusade of modern art in San Diego, which is pretty stolid. A very new city—5 years it's been built up—several bull-dozed developments. Beautiful country though—so mountainous and elegant climate. No smog here.

Oh, and on Friday we went to Pasadena and did a lecture-demonstration at the Playhouse where Rachel Rosenthal is teaching and making a small stir for herself. She says she's on the way to making a big splash, and I know she will, once she sets her mind to it.

We are holding up temperamentally very well together. No fights, no nothing, generally good moods.

There was a party where we stayed, after the performance. The place looks bigger with people in it and smaller without. A 50 foot living room, by the way.

Now flying to San Francisco. What next?

Letter to my parents November 16, 1955, from San Francisco, California:

We performed again last night—biggest house yet and very responsive—laughed in all the right and wrong places and applauded madly. We did much crazy magnetic tape stuff, and they really were quite relaxed about it. I performed pretty well. Afterwards, we went to the Tin Angel, a dive on the waterfront, by invitation of the owner. Jazz band, Remy danced first with Carolyn, then with me, on a raised platform in the back. Great fun. Then we went to Fisherman's Wharf for a fish meal. The other night we ate in a wonderful Chinese restaurant. I am

staying with Susy Burnett, who was at the Gille's [my home in
Paris in 1948] when I was there, also. Very lovely warm person.

San Francisco is a wonderful and beautiful city. All white—
clean—big hills you go up and down and see magnificent views
of the bay, and of the city. Want to live here, just like everyone said. All interesting streets and sections like Paris, some.
Weather never gets colder than early November—and they find
that freezing!

Am saving all programs and reviews, and will deliver them to
you on arrival.

Postcard to my parents, November 18—San Francisco:

> Such excitement here—aren't these reviews superb? [I had
> mailed several reviews along with the postcard.] We are
> all quite frisky after reading them. John chortling all over,
> Merce rather in a daze. The house was almost sold out and
> the audience so warm. Now training north to Portland, OR.
> Nice empty train so far. We are appearing on a TV show in
> Portland—*Banjo* and *Two Step*, and we may be invited back
> to Frisco for a week's run. And do you know, Margot Fonteyn
> did *Swan Lake* the same night and we got all the critics!!

This tour was so exciting and eye-opening for most of us, never
having been to the West Coast before. And it was leisurely enough
so that we could really enjoy the cities we visited, walk around in
them, and get a bit familiar with the ambience. In addition, being
able to perform with some regularity was quite novel—and the enthusiastic reviews we were receiving were extremely rewarding and
morale-boosting.

Another evening, in someone's finished basement, Remy and I
and several dancers were fooling around, joking and generally enjoying ourselves. I was sitting on the edge of a cot and teasing Remy.
He suddenly fell on top of me in a momentary fit of passion. We
hugged and laughed and went back to playing and having fun.

# A Rare Evening of Dances to Music on Tapes

By Alfred Frankenstein

Night before last at the Marines' Memorial Theater, Merce Cunningham, John Cage and their associates reported on the latest in music and the dance as practiced in the New York workshops. The latest seems to be that the modern dance has continued to refine, perfect and extend its well-established techniques, but that music has broken out into the conquest of completely untrodden territory.

We have heard much about the new "musique concrete" in recent years, but this was the first time any of it had been performed in this community. "Musique concrete" is music composed with magnetic tapes, exploiting the infinite possibilities for the transformation of sound which that medium opens up, but remaining faithful to the sounds of the natural world as the source or raw material.

DIMENSIONAL EFFECTS

Some of the music heard Tuesday night employed eight tapes and eight different speakers, thereby creating all manner of dimensional effects, to say nothing of a polyphony so complex as to defy the efforts of an inexperienced ear. Much of the sound that came from the speakers seemed merely raucous, shapeless and haphazard, as music in totally unfamiliar idioms often does; at the same time, it was apparent that this new technique is going places, and that what was presented on this occasion might soon seem as classic in feeling as the early atonal works of Schoenberg seem today.

DANGERS OF METHOD

Cunningham seems already to have sensed a kind of classicism in "musique concrete." At least his "Fragments," to a tape recorder composition by Pierre Boulez, was remarkable for its clarity, precision and sharpness of edge. On the other hand, his "Suite By Chance," to another tape recorder piece by Christian Wolf, seemed to illustrate all the dangers of the method. Chance has always played a larger role in the arts than criticism (especially the artists' own self-criticism) will admit; at the same time, it is possible to force luck too long and too often, whether on the dance floor, in the recording laboratory, or with the dice.

The new music is perhaps the most completely impersonal medium ever invented; the dance, however (and most fortunately) remains inseparable from human beings, and the human creatures of Cunningham's company, like their director, possess both an incomparable range of technique and personalities well worth projecting by means of it. That they are not solely concerned with advanced experiment was shown in a delightful "Septet," to music by Satie, which subjected practically every imaginable form of dancing to very subtle satire but somehow retained a light, consistent style.

## Novel Recital Blends Odd Tape Music and Dancing

By ALEXANDER FRIED

IF YOU like to keep track of what's brand new in the arts, you have a right to kick yourself for not coming out to the Marines Memorial Theater last Tuesday evening.

What took place was a recital of strikingly novel dancing by Merce Cunningham and his New York group. And Composer John Cage took over part of the program for demonstrations of synthetic music emerging from magnetic tape.

Cunningham is a fine, lively and graceful dancer. What's more, he has ideas. His company of four girls and two men, barefoot like himself, don't always match his special skill, but they give him good support.

All his numbers had a stimulating, and often really expressive new approach to solo movement, group patterns, tumblings and slow motions, rushings and writhings, prancings and hoppings and just plain standing still.

The dances were surrealistically strange, but on the whole they were decidedly not foolish. One number used two piano accompaniment (as against magnetic tape accompaniment) and it projected music of Satie with a very nice lyrical tone "at the intersection of joy and sorrow."

In the synthetic music numbers, Cage and his composers and helpers employed four pairs of tape machines and eight loudspeakers and mercifully kept them at quite temperate volume. They had in mind not mere loudness, but rather the mystery and vitality of sound in itself.

It took six people nine months to splice together one four and a half minute tape number, Cage said. The sound effects were clipped from a basic library that seemed to draw on the noises (and sixes) of everything from subway trains, moving nature, muffled voices, fog horns, buzzers, bathwater, escaping steam, Bronx cheers, birds and bagpipes. Some unscheduled effects came into the mixture from the astonished whispers and chuckles of the audience.

By traditional standards, such "music" made no formal sense. Yet for limited periods, it did have touches of mood and anarchic fascination. Whether or not synthetic music has a future, I for one welcomed it on the theory, "I'll try anything once." In fact, I'll gladly try Tuesday's odd experience all over again, if ever again it comes our way.

## Modern Dance Art

### Cunningham Group Fine

By Marjory M. Fisher
The News Music Editor

Dancing as far removed from Russian ballet as the jet age is from the Pony Express delighted a Marines' Memorial Theater audience last night.

The stark simplicity of the modern contrasted vividly with the artificiality of the other. And while Merce Cunningham could certainly outdo any male ballet dancer at his own game, we have yet to see a classic ballet dancer who could match the incredible balance, poise and precision demonstrated by Mr. Cunningham in his modern dance program last night.

#### Superb Balance

He and his excellent associates have made their bodies such precision instruments that they seemed able to do the impossible and hold any stance or posture indefinitely, without a quaver. And when they worked in unison, there was real unity in their ensemble.

Moreover, there was a naturalness and buoyancy in their movements and a rhythmic flow that kept rhythmic patterns going steadily and projecting themselves across the footlights even when there was no music to define and carry it.

#### All Good

Whether in solo work or with his associates—Carolyn Brown, Anita Dencks, Viola Farber, Marianne Preger, Remy Charlip and Bruce King—Mr. Cunningham was the dominating figure. Yet his partners seemed equally skillful.

Their choreography was always interesting and the performance had many exciting moments, even if "Suite by Chance" seemed overly long. Originality, a fine sense of line, and bits of humor added interest and variety.

#### Taped 'Music'

Most humorous was the sound of the recorded tape. (We won't call it music!) It sounded like some hi-fi blow-up of household sounds (like dripping faucets and boiling water) plus barnyard noises, bird songs and bronx cheers! John Cage assured us the "concert" tape was made of sounds recorded at the Library of Congress and it took nine months of splicing to be played on eight machines and eight loud speakers (compliments of Ampex Corporation).

More gratifying was the two-piano work of Mr. Cage and David Tudor.

Newspaper reviews of our San Francisco season, November 1955.

Postcard to my parents, November 19—Portland, Oregon:

Not really a beautiful city from inside. We were on TV yesterday. Tomorrow Civic Theatre—horrible floor on stage. Fun. Ugh.

Postcard, November 20—Portland:

It's a beautiful day today—there is white in the air; sun shining, cold but pleasantly. I walked, went to the museum which was very nice. The central street is lovely with mall and trees.

What I didn't mention in any postcard was that in Portland, Oregon, we performed to a full house (348 seats). Apparently, there were so many patrons that were turned away, that we were asked to perform again the next night, and did. We were popular here. My guess is that the enthusiastic California reviews of Cunningham's dances preceded our arrival in Portland, and made our arrival there an interesting event. Obviously, West Coast audiences had nothing in common with their East Coast cousins.

In Tacoma, we stayed at a woman's house that had a big finished rumpus room in the basement. Merce really let his hair down that evening—perhaps some wine helped—and he ended up by performing a magnificent tap dance sequence for us, drawing on his youthful experience with his tap dance teacher, Mrs. Maude Barrett. (He often quoted her preperformance speech: "Bite your lips, pinch your cheeks, and you're on!") We were wildly appreciative, both of his gorgeous dancing and of his relaxed playfulness. Carolyn, however, had retreated to her room earlier that evening, chagrined by his undignified behavior. Unfortunately, as a result, she missed his rare performance. The next morning was another opportunity for me to urge her to let him off his pedestal, at least on occasion.

Washington was astonishing, with Mount Rainier soaring through the clouds, visible from anywhere in Seattle. We learned that these young western mountain ranges had not been worn down like our older eastern ones, and so they were much bigger and more impressive.

We spent Thanksgiving at Merce's parents' house in Centralia, Washington, the same house he'd grown up in. His parents were very gracious and glad to host us. We met his brothers, proper lawyers like his dad—having a dancer in the family must have taken some getting used to. My most special memory from that occasion was perusing a photo album of Merce's childhood and growing up, and discovering that he was ten years and two days older than I was. From then on, I made and sent him a birthday greeting every year of his life.

Postcard to parents, November 27—Tacoma, Washington:

Carolyn and I sharing a double bed in a house with 3 kids. We're in Tacoma. Got your letter to phone the day after Thanksgiving, I'm sorry—I wanted to phone but there was so much noise at the Cunninghams that you'd never have heard me anyhow.

One night we were driving along a road under towering evergreen trees in a fog so thick that the driver kept his door open in order to keep his eye on the yellow line down the middle of the road. By some great luck, we arrived at our destination safely. Terpsichore, muse of the dance, must have been watching over us.

Postcard to parents, November 29—Tacoma:

Here we are in the bus station going to Bellingham from Tacoma. It has been gorgeous here. Stayed midst enormous Douglas Fir trees, next to a lake. Much silver mist that became very thick at night so you could barely see. We saw a terrible movie last night, but a good one in Portland. [Then the word "Hello," written in Merce's handwriting appears on the postcard] That's Merce. We saw Disney's *African Lion*—beautiful. Remind me to describe the party when Merce soft-shoe danced. He was magnificent.

After our last performance of the tour, we all left in different directions on different timetables. Merce and I were the last two left, and so my last night there, we shared a motel room. You can imagine how thrilled I was to be in such close connection with him. It was a comradely time, quite uneventful aside from the commotion in my heart and head.

# 27

-:-:-:-:-:-:-:-:-:-:-:-:-:-:-

# UPS AND DOWNS
# OF THE DANCERS

In 1956, Remy's first book was published. He was both writer and illustrator. It was titled *Dress Up and Let's Have a Party.*[1] It was a momentous event in his life and therefore in the lives of all of his friends whom he had included in the book. I decided to throw a surprise party for him. All of his friends who were in the book were invited to come in the hilarious costumes he'd illustrated them in. Among those friends were Carolyn, Viola, John Cage, and me. Remy arrived at my apartment door, and when I opened it, dressed exactly as I was in the book, he stared at me and said, "Ohh nooo . . . ," then came in and was overcome with astonishment, delight, and awe at seeing his book come to life. We had a very lively party, and I took a movie of everyone, posed as they were shown in the book. I still have the movie.

Injury and illness were an inevitable aspect of our lives as dancers. There were constant minor injuries: shin splints, stone bruises on the balls of our feet, split skin, blisters, infections, exhaustion. Here's a journal entry from November 30, 1957, after a performance at the Academy of Music in Brooklyn: "Viola had left exhausted, after weeping all through. Merce got sick and went home. Bruce disappeared."

Then there were more serious issues. Just in the years 1957–1958, my journal recorded several illnesses that required time away from dancing. On December 2, 1957: "Viola can't dance for two months—acute anemia. So, mad rehearsal schedule this week to teach Cynthia [Stone]. Impossible." But it turned out not to be impossible: December 3—"Rehearsal, teaching Cynthia *Labyrinthian*. She learns fast." And December 4—"Rehearsal—Cynthia learned all *Labyrinthian* and beginning of *Septet*. Amazing."

Then, March 5—"Cynthia in bed for ten days from accident. How will we get to North Carolina in twelve days? We'll see."

Apparently she made it.

Then Remy's turn: May 12, 1958—"Remy in hospital after four days with 104 degree temperature and measles spots and real illness. . . . Made Remy fine book for hospital get well." May 16—"I went to visit Remy at Manhattan General with cards and flowers from our dance class. We had a lovely hour together. He was feeling somewhat better, growing a beard, hoping to be out on Monday. Had written a beautiful little book about a sinking ship [that little story is part of a book he made later, called *Thirteen*].[2] He was terribly delighted with our book for him, said the drawings were very good."

# 28

-:-:-:-:-:-:-:-:-:-:-:-:-:-

# JOY IN COMPANIONSHIP

In the years I was in the company, we consisted of between six and eight dancers. When we traveled, we included John Cage and David Tudor, Nick Cernovitch (our lighting magician), and Bob Rauschenberg (who could improvise sets in short order). Our travels were filled with much conversation, games, and laughter. The age range among us covered around twelve years, aside from John, who was older. But John was a perennial youngster, so we were basically contemporaries. That contributed to a camaraderie, an easy time relating to and enjoying each other, which we mostly did. We ate dinner together before a performance, were invited to a party, usually, after the concert, where we were well fed, and spent endless hours in the VW bus traveling together, taking turns driving and sitting next to Merce, who was often in the front passenger seat.

When we were in, or near, New York City, our party often included M.C. Richards, Christian Wolff and Earle Brown; Vera and Paul Williams, generous financial supporters of their radical composer friends; and Fance, an artist, and her husband, Louis Stevenson, both devotees of Merce's dancing. Plus, on occasion, other musicians and artists. I have a clear memory of having a conversation with Robert Motherwell, celebrated Abstract Expressionist painter, at one party, though no memory of the content. He was attentive and warm-hearted, easy to connect with.

Some journal entries from the winter and spring of 1957–1958, including several performances, illustrate our amiable connections to each other:

December 16, 1957: "Ready and off to Worcester, MA—Clark University Theatre. Crazy mad hilarious rehearsal all afternoon after lazy lunch and lazy floor warm-ups. Everyone howling and relaxed. Light supper in theatre. The best way, no doubt about it. No rush, relaxed, unstuffed. . . . Remy and I did duet romantically without having spoken of it before. Amazing coincidence and fun like that. Big dinner after. All nine of us piled in VW and off to NYC. Cynthia talked of mental hospital experience as dance therapist. Home at 5:30 A.M." [When I write "home" in these journal entries, I'm referring to my apartment in NYC.]

February 12, 1958, Durham, North Carolina: "Up early, beautifully sunny again but much colder. Big breakfast across the street and took lunch in car. Off we went—learned whist—like bridge only more chance. Remy played my hand with me and we had lots of fun . . . Picnicked in freezing park next to Potomac—wider than Hudson with ice floes. Drove more, whistling and singing. Then napped, enjoyed sunset light on yellow grasses . . . Carolyn drove and we talked intensely about dancing, Merce, then us and our respective choices in handling problem areas."

March 14, 1958: "Woke up at home at 5 AM and took bus to Carolyn's [also in NYC] in slush and snow. Thunder and lightning! End of southern tornadoes. We all took off around 6:30 and after turnpike, snow stopped. . . . We had a jolly time. Nick had ham sandwiches for lunch and steak sandwiches for supper—we ate in the car and didn't stop much. Arrived in Greensboro, NC, at 9:30 P.M. It was very cold. We stayed in a dorm."

March 15: "We were up at 10—sunny cold day—we could see slightly frost-bitten daffodils, budding clusters of red maple leaves, and sparse forsythia blooms (they had snow two weeks ago). They are at least a month ahead of us. Had an enormous steak before rehearsal. Heard some of John and David's music concert after. I always find I like Morty's [Feldman] music—it has such delicacy and exquisiteness from that enormous man—how right. . . . After the dance performance, a reception, Merce holding eloquently forth to rapt followers. Then, all of us dancers out to food and fun in Merce's motel room."

March 16: "After breakfast we left—late—10:30, ate lunch in car. Beautiful sunny day for a while, then grey. Cards and frolic. At Richmond, VA, we took ferry across Chesapeake to some beach. Five hour ride, cold but sunset through cloud layers—rays, pink, purple sea, sea gulls gliding motionless above us and then sliding into a current and disappearing behind us. John was tipsy and hilarious and all of us laughed continually—such a jolly group—they may be insane but they sure can enjoy themselves and get a bang out of life—that's the most sensible insanity I know of. We continued driving with time out for seafood and dragged home at 3:30 A.M."

March 21: "I quote John: 'Welcoming whatever comes.' The Zen idea of giving up desire."

April 16, 1958: "I phone Merce to wish him happy birthday and John answered and was delighted to be reminded. I went to class with present—apples, peaches, relish and a card. Remy and Carolyn had bought him a suitcase."

## PART III

-:-:-:-:-:-:-:-:-:-:-:-:-:-:-

# THE ONLY WAY TO DO IT . . .

# 29

-:-:-:-:-:-:-:-:-:-:-:-:-:-

## SEPARATION MUST COME

Early in 1958, I decided I wanted to have a baby. I was twenty-eight and had been married for a year, to a man with two little boys who lived with their mother but spent weekends and summers with us. Having a baby was a painful decision for me to make, as it meant leaving the dance company, a move that filled me with anguish. I knew that I was about to change my life—I couldn't imagine being a mother and being in the company at the same time, unlike many other dancers. Merce had been invited to bring his dancers to Connecticut College for a summer residency, to teach and perform. It was a major step forward for him, indicating that he was finally becoming well known and respected as an innovative choreographer and fine dancer. I was very happy for him, as I felt it was high time he was beginning to receive the acclaim that he had so long deserved. At the same time, I believed that it would be wrong for me to go with them, learn and perform all the new dances he would choreograph, and then leave the company to give birth. It seemed more ethical to turn my place in the company over to a dancer who would replace me, and who would be able to learn the new works as they were unfolding. So that was my plan, which I communicated to Merce. He was incredibly sweet and loving in all his responses, as I recorded in my journal:

April 11, 1958: "After class, a confab with Merce and John about advisability of breaking in new company member at CT this summer."

April 21: "Took Merce's class—summer still open for me if I want."

May 2: "I had a joyous class with Merce, I am still ambivalent about summer."

May 26: "Merce class and had an emotional scene with him where I said I really couldn't go and he wished I would and said how they'd miss me."

May 29: "When I told Remy about no Connecticut, he said he would cry. That made me sad, too."

June 1: "I feel the coming break with Merce and dancers very heavily and anxiously all over. That I will be less. And I'll just miss them."

June 2: "I went to Limelight [a restaurant in Greenwich Village], Merce was there, said it was too crowded. Isobel [the first company 'manager'—planning tours, etc.] came, we went to Joe's [another eating place], they talked business about Illinois next winter, spring tours, Merce is getting somewhere. By the time he's ready to retire, the public will be up to him. Oh how absurd that such greatness has to be so caught NOW or missed. We went to class by bus, he kept saying I must come this summer—then that I had to tell Marilyn [Wood—to be my replacement], he couldn't. I did and then got terribly sad and weepy. But class was great . . . Then lots of sadness and tears for Merce and nine years of me growing an identity as an artist, a dancer, a part of a group, a not-dilettante, a professional."

June 23: "I went to class. Merce was very sweet, forgot I wasn't going to CT as did Remy. Merce said *Septet* and *Banjo* were mine

In adventurous roles made for me by Merce:

*Above*: In *Galaxy* (1956):
costume by Remy Charlip.
Photograph: Don Drubaker.

*Left*: In *Nocturnes* (1956):
all-white costume by Robert
Rauschenberg. The pre-
miere took place at Jacob's
Pillow. Photographer
unknown.

and not to teach them, that they'd be dropped—I don't *really* think so, but how sweet—and Marilyn would do well but was not me. All the right things. How infinitely kind and loving he can be."

Here are journal excerpts from my last performance with Merce and company, at Ball State Teacher's College in Muncie, Indiana.

July 1: "Up around 8, talked in bed [with Carolyn] until 10. Walked to restaurant for breakfast, David joined Carolyn and me. Campus was very green and cool in shade but hot in sun. At 12:30 we went to auditorium, laid out make-up, warmed up, and rehearsed *Galaxy*. Then watched Merce do new *Collage* [actually the solo from 1952, with music by Pierre Schaeffer]—such amazing parts of feet doing one continuous bounce and arms laying around sharply. Wonderful full way he moves leaving technique far behind—so animal and alive and dynamic. Then Bill [Burdick—in the company just for the year 1958] and Remy came, and went through everything with energy but not the greatest precision. They took movies and photos. Everyone started to menstruate right and left [not the men!].

"We went out to dinner, home to nap and wash and dress up— thence to theatre. Merce was so very sweet and tender—all through this trip but even more before and during performance. Before we left he had said he would bring along his Russian book so we could have a conversation [we were both interested in learning Russian; for me, because I was reading and loving the works of Tolstoy, Dostoevsky, Chekhov, Pushkin. I had also recently heard and loved the Russian song, 'Ochii Chornye,'[1] whose words he sent me years later, merrily illustrated]—such a sweet gesture to make contact. And before the concert he said in French, 'Dance well for me and you and everyone.' And was so extra special in *Septet*. Remy and I did the couple dance like we always wanted to—he was so beautiful and soft and illumined. And then after that inspired end, we went to the dressing room and I bawled my head off and so did Carolyn, and Merce came in and was so tender and said it was not the end and they all loved me and all kinds of things one would like to

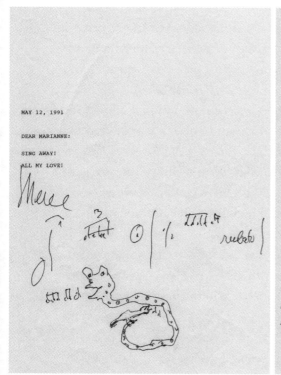

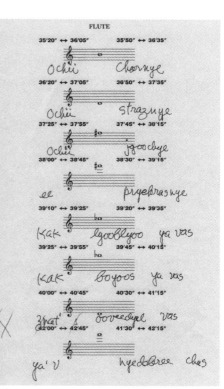

Merce writing to me in playful mode, transcribing and translating the famous Russian song "Ochii Chornye" (Black Eyes). In the 1960s Merce taught himself Russian, though he kept this as one of his many secrets.

hear. Then a reception and then a splendid beer party in a tavern—I had almost two bottles of ale. Merce gave me an envelope of photographs 'to remember us this summer' and a pair of baby pants. And we reminisced about Paris and nine years ago and beginning private lessons with Merce where when he said to jump from second position I couldn't get off the floor so he got behind me and lifted me up. And how he called us 'the kids' when we did *Ragtime Parade*. John said he used to wonder why it was so much nicer to work with us than with the three girls [the three experienced dancers who preceded us in Merce's earliest work]. Finally staggered out and home to bed."

July 2: "Up at 7, bright silvery day . . . Left around 10. In car, got into huge discussion on values with Carolyn, Nick, and some with David, Cynthia and Viola . . . I also had a long questioning of David on his childhood in Philly, playing, success, etc. It was all most interesting, to me at least. Oh, and before that a very good talk with Bill [Burdick] about his training in and giving up of Catholicism. Then a rush to the airfield and half a mile away with two minutes to go—ran out of gas! But we got them a hitch. Stopped for fancy ice cream at an Isaly store in Columbus. Lots of card playing in the afternoon, and at night picnic of broiled chicken in a park with seesaw. Nick talked in Serbian. [That was his ethnicity.] We drove through beautiful hilly country and stopped at Washington, Ohio, in a motel. Carolyn told me stories about The Land [a commune, north of NYC, where John and others lived]—Hultbergs, Williams, David and M.C., Weinribs et al. Awful and chilling [the difficult relationships among them] but the way of the world. David so sweetly apologized for laughing at me during the discussion in the morning. He is so nice."

July 3: "John came in early to hear about yesterday's values discussion. He was wonderful. . . . We breakfasted in diner . . . Then I drove seventy-five miles. John spoke of anarchist communities, how many there were, and of one of the leaders, Benjamin Tucker. [Tucker was a proponent of individualist anarchism in the nineteenth century; toward the end of his eighty-five years of activism, which included producing an anarchist periodical, *Liberty*, he became very pessimistic about the possibility of an anarchist society emerging.]

"Bedford, PA park with pool. Merce, John, Nick, Viola, Cynthia and I swam. Then lunch and taught Cynthia *Nocturnes*. Oh, and during morning stops, taught Merce and Carolyn and Nick and Cynthia *Misirlou, Nebesko Kolo, Tchoukarichka Kolo*, and another folk dance, and we did them at gas stations. [I had learned and then taught Folk Dance at New Lincoln School.] Afternoon napped, more cards, ate remains on Howard Johnson lawn. More cards, I observed Merce's hand in Whist game. Then he was so warm and sweet as we got to New York, and I got lumpy [a lump in my throat] as people unloaded—everyone was very nice. I invited John and David and M.C. to come visit us. Home at midnight."

# 30

-:-:-:-:-:-:-:-:-:-:-:-:-

# FAMILY WINS

That summer, my husband and I rented a little cottage in Bridge-hampton, Long Island, which was a small farming community at that time. My husband's two little boys stayed with us for much of the summer. We swam and played at the beach. We raised veg-etables and flowers, clammed and musseled across the island in Sag Harbor, picked raspberries and blackberries wherever they grew, rescued excellent peaches unbelievably found in the town dump, and canned them. We met a fisherman/chef, Dan Duce, who took my husband fishing and taught me the superb recipe for filet of sole meunière, which I frequently cook to this day. I searched out, picked and served up various edible greens, like purslane and sorrel, which were delicious, as well as dock, which was disgusting. My ed-ible greens investigation came about because Merce had given me the book *Edible Wild Plants of Eastern North America*[1] as a farewell gift from the company. He inscribed it, and the company members, as well as Nick Cernovich, all signed it. It has accompanied me through all my various moves.

In August, I voyaged across the Long Island Sound to see the Merce Cunningham Company dance performance at Connecticut College, the culminating event of their six-week residency. Here are my journal entries for August 14 and 15, 1958:

8/14 New London: A friend picked me up and took me to the theatre. I had brought a huge bouquet of flowers, went into the theatre to put my flowers in water, and met Remy. Such a greeting ensued! I was considerably excited and shaking and decided to forget about dinner and, instead, stay with the dancers. Everyone was so welcoming and warm and having had a marvelous summer, with Merce as sweet as could be. He had a huge devoted following of students, complete with mash notes, etc. He and Remy both lost weight, but looked wonderful. I was so happy to see them, and I was so full of emotion. Recital—Fantastic. *Antic Meet*—hilarity communicated through movement and timing, rather than through story-telling, evoking so much of the mixed and rapid feelings one has in life only much stronger and more concentrated and more exciting. Beautiful unity of costuming, dance, form; excellent performances, music having its own life but of the same nature as the dance, and adding much comedy. Tremendous subtlety, especially in Merce's beautiful little soft-shoe solo, costumed in overalls, so delicate and reminiscent and tender and sweet and moving. In the company, wonderful sharp precision of movement and timing, swift unexpected changes and breaks in continuity, built up absurdities like Remy and Marilyn 'swimming' and getting tangled up. Comedy on such a level: Viola sitting still so long, then cracking up the audience by turning her head; Merce and Carolyn's bedroom duet so elegant and tender and ridiculous; the orgiastic bursts of group movement—magnificent discombobulation of space that rocked the stage; Viola's foot under that umbrella of fireflies. So much beauty in all the comedy and so much dignity in fallibility, like the human condition. Ah.

The rest of the program by other choreographers and dancers—junk. [As I have mentioned, my concept of dance was intractably formed by the nine years in Merce's company.] Afterwards, a visit with Merce; stayed in Carolyn's room and we talked and gossiped late.

8/15 Up at 7, breakfast, and two magnificent classes with Merce and his hordes of students in an enormous gym. They applauded endlessly after each class. I loved taking the classes and felt wonderful moving: plunged into everything as totally and vigorously as possible—barely lasted. Afterwards, I went to hear Morty's [Feldman] music. Lunch, followed by a rehearsal on stage of *Nocturnes*—a world of enchantment—breathtakingly

*Left to right*: Valda Setterfield, Merce, and me, at Connecticut College, 1958. I had recently left the company to start a family; this was my first visit to my old colleagues. Valda, new to the company then, remained into the 1970s. Photograph: Marion Rice, Carolyn's mother.

beautiful and harmonious and romantic. Having always been a participant in the dance, and never a spectator, I had no idea. Seeing his work is a revelation—his dances offer an important insight—so vast and so clear—one can see through the dancing to the concept of vastness behind—there is much of individualness of incidents, and coincidence, of singleness, and relationship of nature and movement and pulsing life, enduring life, ambiguous inconsistent and unanswerable life and lyrical beauty.

Then to see a rehearsal of a new dance: *Summerspace*—again I was floored. I thought of birds on the lawn, and afterwards Merce said exactly that. It is fast and tightly constructed and has also great explosions of movement—it ends on one.

After many tender farewells, I left and got on the ferry, writing notes on the dances.

What I don't mention in the journal is a humorous moment that occurred just before I left the dancers. They urged me to stay and see the performance that night. I said, with great confidence, that I had to go back because I had to get pregnant that night. They laughed, but I was right—I did!

# 31

-:-:-:-:-:-:-:-:-:-:-:-:-:-

# THE CONNECTION HOLDS

During the next two years, while I still lived in New York City, I had many interactions with Merce, with the company, and on occasion with John and David. It was extremely satisfying to maintain relations with them, to take class sometimes, and to teach my parts in various dances to other dancers.

September 9, 1958: "Merce and Remy came to our home for a lovely evening. We showed the dance movies [movies I and my husband had taken of various dances]; Merce was fascinated and disturbed and curious." [These movies were donated to the Cunningham company.]

November 3: "Went to Dance Players Studio and secretaried for Merce, who was so sweet and loving, and said he and Carolyn had a present for me. They really do not forget, and that loyalty is very rare, I find. And I revel in it."

November 4: "To Merce's studio to register beginners."

November 15: "Early off to The Land. Merce, Carolyn, Remy in the back seat. Merce and Carolyn gave me a beautiful lace cap and bib from Belgium [Merce and Carolyn had had their first European dance minitour earlier], and cologne. Remy brought his new book. It was a lovely ride out. Remy so brown and healthy looking from Puerto Rican vacation.

"Interesting place—attractive modern very convenient houses, mostly grouped around a center plot. Much windows. All had lunch at Vera's [Williams]. Like a native community where everyone cares for all children. Only thirty-five minutes to the [George Washington] bridge!"

December 15: "I went to dance class with Carolyn teaching—it was fine and she's very good and runs a lovely lively class."

December 22: "I went to beginning of Merce's Christmas course [of classes]—some thirty people! Biggest private class the Master has ever had."

January 3, 1959: "Carolyn Brown's [Merce Cunningham] Dance Company dinner: [Bob] Rauschenberg reflecting on my review of Paul Taylor's concert [printed in *The Village Voice* newspaper[1]], concluded with a personal tribute that surprised and touched me."

Here is a copy of the Paul Taylor review Bob was referring to:

*At the 92nd Street YMHA, Saturday evening, December 19.*
   "It is three years since Paul Taylor started performing solo and group dances, and one of the most invigorating things about his concerts has been the constant development and change from one year to the next. Not that one always prefers the new work—in this case I didn't—but it is important that an artist keep growing.
   In Taylor's earlier concerts I was struck by the joy emanating from dancers and dances. This is gone, and has not been replaced by anything of equal force—no greater complexity of space, rhythm, dynamics, or greater veriety of movement, or

increase in atmosphere, except in two works from last year's concert: "Epic" and particularly "Events 2." The latter is a tremendously poetic interpretation of a "slice of life"—two girls waiting—and has intense atmosphere, created by the economy of movement, the stillness, a recording of rain sounds, and wind blowing skirts and curtains. It is an original theatrical experience.

As a dancer, Mr. Taylor is vigorous, supple, and beautiful to watch. His company of girls . . . are well trained and lovely, and all maintain the expression of quiet serenity which seems at present to be the attitude of the dances.

I look forward to future concerts and the interesting developments they should present in Paul Taylor's choreographic career.

One of the side benefits of dancing in Merce's company was securing a gig as dance critic for *The Village Voice*. It happened via my familiar experience with serendipity. I was at a party one evening in 1955 when I met Ed Fancher. He told me he was starting a newspaper that would be called *The Village Voice*. I cheerfully volunteered to be a dance critic for the new paper. He was delighted and immediately acquiesced. I continued in that capacity until 1959. I enjoyed watching performances as a thoughtful reviewer as well as observing them as a dancer. The combination was new and stimulating.

January 21: "Went to Merce's class and had a good time. Talked to him quite a while after, and gave him an apparently astounding and delicious insight—that he got upset when he was tired because it released adrenalin to keep him going. He loved that—said he'd never think of it because it might be coddling himself—an excuse. But he felt this was true. Admitted that after all these years, he still doesn't *know* the dance he's choreographing will come out fine. He talked about staging it around the orchestra. Then I watched their first full run-through of the dance. [This must have been either *Gambit for Dancers and Orchestra* or *From the Poems of White*

*Stone*, to be performed at the University of Illinois at Urbana, where Merce had a three-month residency. Both those dances premiered in 1959.] It was so exciting—great complexity of his. Marvelous group work with weaving and breaking and together and apart and then solos of his and Carolyn's and adagio interludes. It was danced, too. [This refers to the fact that sometimes run-throughs were just marked, or indicated, by the dancers, rather than fully danced.] And such use of music—interchange and independence and yet a definite connection. Afterwards I cheered loudly and beamed about it and seemed to generally make them all encouraged. Merce spoke of making it 'nasty' in places. Like the fights in a dance-hall, he said he thought of it as. And when I said it was a high-tension dance he was so pleased—thought it too slow and dull! What an image he has of it."

April 20: "Merce got a Guggenheim, so I phoned him."

My baby was born late in May of 1959, so my attention became happily focused on motherhood. But some time in the following year, I did teach one of my parts to Marilyn Wood, while my baby crawled around on the dance floor.

# 32

-:-:-:-:-:-:-:-:-:-:-:-

# LEAVING NEW YORK,
# BUT NOT OUR BOND

In the fall of 1960, our family moved out of New York City to Lido Beach, Long Island; in 1965 to Philadelphia, and in 1969 to Amherst, Massachusetts. I maintained my connection to Carolyn, Remy, and Merce no matter where I lived and no matter how much time passed.

In fact, in May of 1961, by which time I had a two-year-old daughter and a six-month-old son, I paid a visit to Merce in New York City with my two little ones in tow. Here is the journal entry:

> Merce was so warmly welcoming, loved Matthew and played with him. Julianna hid behind my skirts for a while. Soon took off shoes and socks and ran and danced.

And a year later, March 30, 1962:

> In the afternoon I took Matthew to Merce's rehearsal of
> *Aeon*—a long, rambling, beautiful, difficult dance. The reward
> is always in the large group sections. The sudden simultaneity,
> explosion of space and rhythm are so exciting. Matthew was
> great at the rehearsal. Lots of noises to enjoy, echoes, running
> about the aisles, imitation of dancers. And he kissed Merce—
> after first offering to—twice!

The next day, without child: "Off to Merce concert. Very exciting.
*Aeon* in epic tradition, but tighter and more consistently beautiful.
*Crises* stunning and solid, great jazzy music. *Antic Meet* as always delicious. Party afterwards. I do so enjoy being with everyone, loving
the dancers, helping to feed them."

My desire to stay connected to Merce, despite leaving the company, was shared by Merce also. He made a point of keeping in
touch with me, periodically writing me very affectionate letters and
postcards, some of which I have included here.

When my children grew older, I would attend his concerts whenever possible, greeting my old friends John Cage, David Tudor, and
David Vaughan. I would always go backstage afterward to visit with
Merce. He was inevitably very warm and welcoming, and he usually would regale me with some funny memory of my time in the
company, such as the story I recounted at the very beginning of this
memoir: how I dropped a smoking ball on stage at a Jacob's Pillow
performance in the 1950s, practically giving Ted Shawn (the propri-
etor) a nervous breakdown.

In February 1970, the Cunningham Company performed at the
University of Massachusetts in Amherst, where we had just moved.
I was very excited at the prospect of seeing them perform in my new
hometown. I was interviewed on the radio about Merce's dances
and my experience in the company. I also took both my daughter
and my son out of school, and with the permission of the company,

กรุงเทพฯ    คลาดน้ำในคลองสี่แยกเทาขวด
H. W. &
No. 47 BANGKOK, THAILAND: Scenery of the floating market.

Where are you going, my pussi
I'm going to Bangkok to
the Queen, & well0! King
too. & they saw us. and
talked with us, and no
wonder the people like
them. She was wearing gold
and dusk-colored orange
& diamonds. "I how heard you
have great success all over Europe."
Love Merce

Marianne Simon
28 Bath St.
Lido Beach, New York

---

Everyday I look at
your photograph
with Juliana, &
today you looked
more radiant than
usual — as for
Juliana, it's
not fair!
my love to you, Merce

Marianne Simon
28 Bath St.
Lido Beach,
New York

U.S. POSTAGE 3¢ LIBERTY

NEW YORK N.Y.
FEB 21
4-PM
1961

Emmett Stenders

Size 303s

---

C 129
Dear all of you: on
the Lido in Venice
my last chip at the roulette
table came up a winner.
Last night, Carol and I lost
10 Kronor (82.00) at the
slot machines in the Tivoli
amusement park. But we
are all well, even after 4
weeks of performing in
London! Hope you are too.
Stockholm! IX·5·64      Love to you,
Merce

The Simons
28 Bath St.
Lido Beach,
New York
USA.

35- SVERIGE

STOCKHOLM
5.9.64

Printed in England by Henry Stone & Son (Pridsey) Ltd., Banbury

British Museum    nineteenth century    Mughal School    THE STANDING ELEPHANT    (Size 5½ in. high)

FLYGPOST
PAR AVION

St. John's Church was erected in 1741. In this building in 1775 Patrick Henry gave his famous "Give me liberty or give me death" speech. The illustration is reproduced from a painting executed by William Paxton for The Life Insurance Company of Virginia.

THE STONE PRINTING & MFG. CO., ROANOKE, VA., U.S.A.

THREE CENTS POSTAGE

POST CARD

Dear Marianne

Happy Birthday to you! Love

Merce

10/18/86

I saw Matt in Boston. He looks fine!

11/3/88

Dear Marianne;
Here to you and thank you for helping us. We had a fine season at The Joyce Theatre, and are shortly off to Brazil for a 2 week tour. — Rio, São Paulo and Belo Horizonte. Several of the dancers are staying for a vacation, but I just look forward to coming home and sitting down.
Hope you all are well — and as ever
Merce

*Facing page and following pages*: Missives from Merce, 1960–1995, with songs, dances, birds, and animals. Reading these, I find it wonderful to see that my affection for Merce was matched by his for me. He refers to John (Cage), Matt (my son, Matthew), Julianna (my daughter), and Carol (as we often called Carolyn Brown). Though some are written after John Cage's death in 1992, Merce's spirit shines on unchanged.

Dear Marianne
As always, it was wonderful
to see you. Thank you
for putting up with Eliot
(me?) I heard you
laughing a lot.
all my love.
Mere

NEW YORK, NY
PM
14 AUG
1989
U.S. CUSTOMS SERVICE
200TH ANNIVERSARY
1789 – 1989
Buffalo Bill Cody
USA 15

Marianne Simon
P. O. Box 58
1 Chestnut Plain Rd.
Whately, Mass.
01093

Happy Birthday!

Dear Marianne —
John once said you were the
heart of our company —
How right he was!
Love to you and Mille Fois
fêtes to come —
Mere

July 19, 1994

Dear Marianne:  A present for you:

### SONG FOR A CONTEMPORARY CHANTEUSE

I'M  BIO    I'M BIO

I'M  BIO    DEGRADABLE

YOU MAY NOT BELIEVE IT

BUT IT'S NOT DEBATABLE

WITHOUT PHOSPHATES

IT'S NEVER TOO LATE

YOU CAN BE AIDABLE TOO

OH IT'S  BIO   IT'S BIO

IT'S REALLY REBATABLE

SO  GRAB YOUR HEART

GET A REAL START

BE  BIODEGRABLE TOO.

*love,*

*From your composer*

*friend*

*Merce*

---

April 19, 1995

*Dear Marianne:*

*I remember it all as though it were just
around the corner, and you got to encore
Rag Time Parade.*

*We were in Taipei giving four shows last
week, and the fourth was on Easter Sunday
which also happened to be my birthday (76)
and there I was "trodding the boards".*

*And yesterday was your birthday, love to
you and many cakes and candles.*

*Now we are in NYC for a few weeks, and I
and my two cats are contending with workmen
over our heads repairing our skylight, badly
in need of same. It will get done, but the
drilling and hammering after a 22 hr. flight
Taipei to my abode, are pushing the boundaries.
The cats are more used to it than I am, having
had a week of it ahead of me.*

*Love, love to you.*

Merce

55 Bethune St.  NY  NY 10014

allowed them to watch dance rehearsals, the stage set-up, the music rehearsals, and gave them free rein to hang out with all the dancers.

The postperformance reception took place at the Lord Jeffery Inn, on the campus of Amherst College, in the center of town. I had written a tongue-in-cheek song in the company's honor, to the tune of *The Frozen Logger*, an old folk song.[1] I sang it at the reception, and it was received with much hilarity, to my great satisfaction.

There was also a splendid dance company visit to our family's farm in the Adirondacks, April 22, 1973. The dance company, which by then was very large and traveled by bus (not a microbus, but a macrobus: a regular full size bus), had been performing in Saranac Lake, New York. Having learned that they were in the vicinity, we invited them to come spend the afternoon with us. The bus appeared, driving slowly down our long dirt road. When it arrived in front of our farmhouse, the door opened and the dancers emerged and fanned out in wonder, all around our fields. It was like the release of a vast array of butterflies. It was a gorgeous, very moving scene that I've never forgotten. The dancers were all living in New York, and besides, they had been cooped up in the bus while touring. It was not surprising that they would be filled with awe and relief amidst all our green space.

In March 1975, Merce's company was to perform at Williams College. That was an hour away from where we lived, so we eagerly went to see the performance. It was in the Lasell gymnasium on the second floor basketball court. We arrived early, sat in the grandstands and were able to watch the company rehearsing. When Merce came out onto the court, I dashed down from our seats, and tackled him with great delight and affection. He laughed heartily at the enthusiastic greeting and welcomed me with equal enthusiasm. This vigorous greeting was emblematic of my conviction that he deserved to be treated as a beloved friend, not an untouchable god.

In March 1978, the dance company returned to the University of Massachusetts, with many new members. The performance was wonderful, as always. Afterward, the entire company was invited to

With Merce, Dallas, Texas, October 1987. Photograph: Carolyn Brown. Carolyn and I joined Merce and his company there when he received the Algur H. Meadows Award for Excellence in the Arts.

our house, where we fed them, and the dancers listened with rapt attention as Merce, John, and I reminisced about the early days in the company. They had never had a chance to hear that much history. Later, John washed dishes with my second husband, the artist Tom Leamon. (Tom has had the honor of having one of his paintings accepted by the Smithsonian Air and Space Museum. It's from a series of his WWI paintings of famous pilots, and that particular painting is of Charles Guynemer, a French flying hero.) John kept asking questions about Tom's life, and after hearing each answer, he would reply, "That's nice." Tom imitates John to this day.

In October of 1987, Merce was to receive the Algur H. Meadows Award for Excellence in the Arts, in Dallas, Texas. Carolyn, who had left the company in 1972, and I both flew to Texas for the splendid event. The dance company was in residence; there were

*Left:* Again with Merce, Dallas, October 1987. Photographer unknown.

*Below:* The letter I received from Merce after we met in Dallas.

XII/7/87

Dear Marianne,

John's *Europera 1 + 2* hasn't happened yet! 3 days before the original opening, Nov 12, the stage burnt up. Sad and chaotic. Now it's supposed to open this Sat, 12th & I'm going to Frankfurt again. John bore the disaster bravely, only saying it was harder on many of the others than himself.

I loved being with you in Dallas. It was a treat for me, and such a relief from the rituals. I'm grateful to-&-/ to you for being there. Hope all is well. Much love to Tom & you

Merce

*Left to right:* Merce, me, Tom Leamon (my second husband, behind sofa), and the musician David Tudor, 1990, Amherst. Photographer unknown.

performances and symposia. There was even a dinner for which we dressed in evening wear. Carolyn and I were on two panels: one about the company at Black Mountain in the summer of 1953, moderated by David Vaughan; the other about dancing for Merce. It was a wonderful reunion, and two photographs memorialized it, as well as the appreciative letter I received from Merce upon my return home.

In 1990, the Cunningham Dance Company performed again in Amherst, with a party following the performance at the home of one of the dancers. There, a photo was taken of Merce, a happy me, David Tudor, and my husband Tom kneeling behind the couch.

As three of my granddaughters reached the age of nine, they became interested in all the photos of Merce around the house, and in the stories I told about dancing with him. I decided they had to see his dances and certainly they had to meet him. Two of them, Rosie and Lizzie, were nine years old in 1998, so I took them to Jacob's Pillow in August to watch their first dance concert. (Rosie

Merce with my granddaughters Lizzie and Rosie. Jacob's Pillow, August 1998.

Merce, me, and my granddaughter Sophia. Dartmouth College, October 2007.

was the daughter of my stepson from my first marriage; Lizzie was the daughter of my stepdaughter from my second marriage.) They were thrilled. Afterward we went backstage and they met the master, who was delightful with them and they with him. My youngest granddaughter, Sophia, turned nine in 2007, so off we went to Dartmouth College in October 2007 to watch another performance. Once again, Merce was so sweet to her, and she was very excited by the dancing.

It turned out that Lizzie (Feidelson) later interned with the Cunningham Foundation, took Cunningham classes and became a lovely dancer herself in New York. What a joy to pass that on.

# 33

-:-:-:-:-:-:-:-:-:-:-:-:-:-

## PARIS CALLS AGAIN

In January 1998, the Cunningham company was engaged to perform at Opéra Garnier in Paris, a very impressive venue: a large, historic, magnificent theater, and an iconic symbol of Paris. Carolyn and I decided to spend the week in Paris. The company administrative director enabled us to fly first class by giving us his extra miles (he hated flying and didn't go himself). We planned to attend three of the performances as well as the elegant party thrown in Merce's honor by Judith Pisar. She was a Merce Cunningham Dance Company board member, who resided in Paris. Merce was deeply grateful for our presence there, we who loved him and had accompanied him years earlier on his artistic journey. (His life companion, John Cage, had died in 1992.) Merce was very expressive, both physically and verbally, about his pleasure in our company.

Journal excerpts from Paris, January 1998:

Friday, January 9: "[After getting lost several times] finally found Opéra [Garnier] just at 7:30 and were given two seats, third row center! I had a very tall man in front of me who perfectly bisected the stage, but by moving back and forth, I got the whole picture. We saw *Rune*; *Garnier Event I*, which consisted of [parts of three dances:] *Run* (from *Dime-a-Dance*), *Suite for Five*—finally [I hadn't seen any part of it since I was in the company]—I watched my part and some of it felt very familiar, and *Winterbranch*; the last dance was the new piece, *Scenario*—brilliant bright lighting, costumes padded every which way, and bare arms and legs cavorting in all directions. *Rune* was a fine dance, and *Winterbranch* is such a knockout.

"Afterwards, we went to Restaurant Olympe at rue St. Georges and had a feast. Merce came and sat next to me and was so pleased we were here and chattered away all through dinner about old times and dance. Quoted M.C. [Mary Caroline Richards] when he once told her his feet hurt, and she said something like 'of course, they should,' which he thought very funny, and thinks of often—so he never complains. He was very sweet and affectionate and talkative. Other people there were Carolyn, David Vaughan, Sage Cowles and Sue Weil, both of Walker Art Center—Sage was at ballet school with Merce, and Sue Weil is currently on his board; David Guion [Merce's Development person] and Stephen Shelley,[1] assistant company manager and Merce's 'crutches'—takes Merce wherever he needs to go. [By this time, Merce's arthritis made it difficult for him to walk and get around].

"Taxi home and bed at 2:30."

Saturday, January 10: "Carolyn read a poetic and very favorable review of opening night Merce."

"Another Opéra night . . . Took #29 bus this time—had to wait twenty minutes but it came and we got to Opéra in about ten minutes. This time we had free tickets to a box facing the stage, right in the center. Bénédicte Pesle, Merce's French promoter, was in it with us, plus some friends—a Japanese musician and a French woman. This was such a different view from last night—the entire stage visible at once. Same program, different cast. Foofwa d'Imobilité [the new stage name of Frédéric Gafner] danced *Rune*—he is so gorgeous. Carolyn was thrilled with *everything*, which is rare for her. At the end of *Scenario* she was in tears and so relieved because she wanted to *feel* in love with the dances, so she could write from that place.

"It is so moving at the end of *Scenario*, when the entire cast of fifteen is lined up for curtain call, all in bright red, and then Merce comes out in his Comme Les Garçons black suit, and everyone in the audience roars their appreciation and devotion to this brilliant, always new, crippled choreographer, once the greatest dancer. With his fuzzy white halo and happy smile. Many curtain calls, audience on its feet.

"This perspective for seeing the dances was wonderful—to see it all in one glance. Gorgeous. And I never knew what an elegant piece *Suite* was. It was fun to 'feel' some of the movements that I used to do, as I watched.

"Also this opera house is *so* magnificent, so ornate, everything carved with statues in every niche and corner and edge. A big Chagall painting in the center of the ceiling of the performance auditorium, and baroque paintings on the ceiling of the lobby. Big staircases, plush lined boxes, the orchestra seats roomy. And the most ornate rehearsal room imaginable backstage.

"We went backstage with David Vaughan and Stephen Shelley and Bénédicte Pesle. Carolyn cried on Merce's shoulder—he certainly felt her profound appreciation and told her he loved her. This time I hung back until she had her time with him—it seemed very important. Then he greeted us all. He went on home with Stephen, who has been at this demanding job for three and a half years. His interest is in directing his own theater pieces and he's taking needed time away from it to be Merce's factotum. But he sounds ready to move on. What an on-call job he has.

"Former company member Emma Diamond had arrived from England with a friend, and wanted a little dinner party. So David Vaughan, Carolyn, Michael Cole, who is leaving the company after the Dieppe performance to study computers and assure his financial future, Emma and her friend, and I all went to dinner—we stopped in four or five brasseries on Boulevard [des] Capucines till we found one that had only a thirty minute wait for a table. We met Frédéric Gafner and his mother in one—she trained him as a dancer, just like Carolyn and her mom. (At the theater, before we left, Carolyn had a chance to tell Frédéric how wonderful he was.)

"Michael and Emma were so sweet, wanting to hear stories of old times. I felt more at ease with Michael—he was so warm and gracious and attentive—than with many of the others who all know Carolyn well and me hardly at all. The talk was all about Merce and dancing—Emma was one who left during the tyrannical and traumatic reign of Art Becofsky [former company manager]. Twelve people left over two years, before David brought in an outside consultant who listened to everyone and then said 'Art has to go.'

"Carolyn told about the company meltdown during the six-month first world tour. Bob Rauschenberg had just won the Venice Biennale, so everywhere the company went, John and Merce were unknown by the press, but Bob was mobbed. Merce withdrew from everyone in his version of a snit, including from John, who then got hurt in turn, while Bob, who was very playful, engaged with the company. More miff, and he got a talking-to by John: seducing the dancers, etc. Bob was also mounting well-received events, etc. So a bunch of dancers left the company after they got home. There was more to this tale of intrigue—it will be in Carolyn's book."

Monday evening, there was a reception for Merce at the elegant Paris home of Judith Pisar, a Merce Cunningham Dance Company board member. Carolyn was dressed in blue, and I was dressed in red. It turned out that we were the only guests in color—everyone else was in black.

Journal entry, Monday, January 12, at Pisar's reception: "I very much enjoyed talking with Foofwa Frédéric, first with Carolyn and then myself, speaking of his plans. He's 28, needing to find what is inside himself. He loves to write, wants to find his own choreography. Because of his genius as a dancer, he has offers on faith, apparently, to do choreography. His mother is Brazilian, was a leading dancer in the de Cuevas ballet, his father was in the corps. His mom went on to teach, and taught him from very early, so at fourteen he was performing. Danced three years with the Stuttgart Ballet. Father became a photographer, lives now in Paris, mom in Geneva. He grew up in Geneva.

"Merce said that the first day he saw Frédéric in class, he said, 'Whoever that is, give him a scholarship.' Frédéric has wonderful confidence. Said he chose Foofwa as a name because it's sort of Dada, and everyone is fou [crazy, in French], and the d'Imobilité is 'kind of ironic.'

"I went out on the terrace by myself, which motivated several dancers to come out—I recognized Thomas Caley and Banu Ogan. Introduced myself and asked [Banu] about her Turkish background. [My sister-in-law has lived in Turkey for fifty-plus years, so I was very interested.] Her family left Ankara for US when she was two, but they go back to Istanbul every couple of years, and she 'feels' Turkish. We talked a little about *Suite*. Then I went in (to get away from the cigarettes!) and someone said 'Merce wants to talk to you.' So I sat down on the floor at the foot of his chair and he squeezed my hand and expressed his delight at my coming over. Pointed out the large mushy Philip Guston [painting] over the couch and the large elegant Ad Reinhardt over the stairway. [Both artists were Abstract Expressionists, working in New York. Philip Guston was my art teacher for one semester at New York University, in 1951. I produced a large pointillist painting for him.]

"There was a gift to Merce of a John Cage five-minute non-prepared piano piece called *The Dream*, from 1948, which Merce had done a solo to, played by a pianist—played it beautifully. Sounded very Satie-esque, but rhythmically quite different. Merce told stories about it to everyone—about how John had to do very little preparing of the piano when accompanying Merce in performances because he had only a few minutes between pieces to change the preparation. After John stopped accompanying Merce with his pieces, he got into much more complex preparation.

"Then Merce wanted Carolyn to join us, so she did. And he kept saying how happy he was that we were there. At one point, I said, 'It's so exciting' and he said, 'Oh it's much more than that,' and a moment later, I saw tears on his face. So we stayed with him all the rest of the evening. Someone took a group photo, I took a photo of him, one of him and Carolyn, and she took one of him and me.

"He spoke again of how his brothers reacted when he spoke in Seattle—one brother said, 'Well, you read that speech without your glasses,' and the other one said, 'Why don't you do pieces that please the public?' But he said his father understood something: he [Merce's father] said, 'I don't know about your dance game but I do know you work very hard.' He apparently felt acknowledged by that. Plus [he told] about how his father was content with his mother's frequent traveling, 'because she always brings home little trinkets,' and she loves to do it.

"He reminisced with Carolyn and me. He asked me how we met and I told him the story. He remembered that I was in the class [in Paris] and that the studio looked out over a Russian church.

"When we were getting ready to go, I was standing with Merce, [Carolyn was, too] and his dancers were enjoying seeing him with us, and he told them, 'Whenever I see that last position in the Trio of *Suite*, I see Marianne doing it. Also those turns with the leg swing, oh, so beautiful.' I told him when I saw Derry [Swan] doing those turns, I could feel it inside.

"And he also told Carolyn, when remembering her last concert, in Paris, how he almost cried but thought, because everyone was crying, 'If I cry, the whole company will fall apart.' So he didn't. And how John rushed back after playing for the concert, saying, 'Did I do it well?' wanting it to be *specially* good for her last performance.

"We three took a taxi together—he gave us 200F to pay for it, as his 'gift' to us. We dropped him off at his hotel, and then went on home."

Carolyn Brown, Merce, and me in the foreground; six members of the Cunningham board behind us. Paris, January 1998.

From the same January 1998 series: Carolyn and Merce, photo by me; me and Merce, photo by Carolyn.

Journal entry, Tuesday, January 13: "Last night, some woman—maybe Suzanne Gallo, the costumer—told Carolyn that all the dancers were afraid of her, because she'd been such a star. Carolyn couldn't get it, until I asked her how she felt when she met Margot Fonteyn. And Jared [Phillips] was reported to have said of Carolyn, from the videos, 'she could do anything we do now. She was a true star.' And she is *so* modest about taking any of that in. She says she doesn't identify with 'that person' at all.

"Also, David Vaughan and Michael Cole entertained at the [Pisar] party last night with a very amusing patter song—David very earnest, Michael cracking up once. David apparently performs with Al Carmines at clubs and events!"

Journal entry, our last performance: "Our seats were first row mezzanine on the side. After the first piece the two Davids [Vaughan and Guion] came over and apologized for our seats and gave us theirs in exchange, which were in the center! We are coddled!

"I saw *Installations* for the first time. It was wonderful. And the music was terrific—acoustic hand-made gongs, etc. all in the front boxes and in the balcony, so the sound was all around, and run by computer so no one was playing them—just the composer in the pit! The set was Elliot Caplan's three video sets showing slow, slow, still and moving body parts. Very beautiful.

"The second dance was a world premiere of *Pond Way*, a breathtakingly beautiful piece. A huge blow-up of a Roy Lichtenstein very delicate black and white dots making a Chinese-inspired land and water scene with a tiny boat in color in the lower left hand corner. A Chinese woman explained in the morning tour [we had gone on a tour of the Opéra Garnier the previous day] that the human is always tiny in the landscape because the Chinese recognize the tiny part of the universe that humans are. Costumes all white with cutaway sleeves and legs so everything flowed and wafted. Fluid, lots of very slow, soft movements as well as sudden fast or sharp ones. Lovely eastern sounding music—the whole was so unified. Merce said several times how he was as nervous before this new piece as he was before his first solo. But when I talked to several dancers afterward, they said he gave them an A OK signal as they exited the wings. And he got a roaring response to the dance.

"The last piece was another *Event*, drawn from *Torse*, *Pictures*, three duets from different pieces and a grand finale from *Points in Space*. The set was from *Points in Space*—sort of expressionist canvas on back and one side. Dancers in black unitards. I was very sleepy by then so didn't take it all in. The music I didn't like—jazz saxophonist Steve Lacy, and Takehisa Kosugi doing his mixture of stuff—it wandered around and never stopped. Another standing ovation at the end, with some rhythmic ensemble clapping by the audience.

"Reception in the Foyer de la Danse, behind the stage. Beautiful spread of hors d'oeuvres and little pastries and endless champagne. I talked with Elliot Caplan [the filmmaker],[2] who said he was let go after twenty years with the company—no money. He's anxious. Has two projects in front of him to tide him over the beginning. But is very sad, wrenchingly so, to leave the company—his family. [Happily, Elliot Caplan's creativity led to an illustrious international career, with many awards for his films and videos, numerous exhibitions, and film-making all over the world.]

"Went over to where Merce was and stood next to him while he talked to people. He looked much better than when we ran into him backstage this morning, when he looked totally exhausted.

"During the reception, they raised the curtain at the front of the stage so there was this glorious perspective from the mirrored back of the Foyer all the way to the end of the auditorium, with its maroon plush colored fauteuils [large chairs] with a gold crest on each. Those do not fold up."

After all that, we decided to go out and eat with some friends, among whom was Jackie Matisse Monnier, granddaughter of Henri Matisse, daughter of Pierre Matisse, and stepdaughter of Marcel Duchamp! According to my journal, "Her mother was introduced

2.1.98

Dear Marianne:

Thank you for your wonderful letter. One of the
best parts of those two weeks were my moments with
you and Carolyn and Sage and Sue. It helped me
survive the rest.

Those two weeks remain as a kind of movie about
theatre, so full of exaggeration, but also warmth
and amazement. We had a one night stand in Dieppe,
smaller theatre, but same enthusiasm and there was
a gorgeous sea to look at, and a seagull came and
perched on my hotel window sill. Friendly.

We came back from a one night stand in Burlington
on Friday. A 7-hour bus ride up, a 90' Event in
the Flynn theatre, a 7-hour bus ride back, but
through such handsome country. Vt. is surely one
of the handsomest of the states, and to another
warm, interested if with some puzzlement, audience.

Now I am sitting at the computer writing this to
you and Blotch, my black and white cat, just
decided to jump off my lap and lie on the floor
in the sunshine pouring through the windows.

It was wonderful you were there, and after so
many years when you were there too.

All my love,

Merce

101 West 18th st.
NY   NY   10011

Merce wrote me this letter after Carolyn and I had spent a week in Paris with
him and his dancers in January 1998. His bird drawings were always a treat.

to Marcel by Max Ernst and Dorothea Tanning because they disap-
proved of the rich men she was dating"!!

At the end of the meal, the waiter said, "'If you sing me a song,
you don't have to pay the bill'—so I promptly began singing, *À
La Claire Fontaine,* and *Aux Marches du Palais.* The waiter was

apparently deeply touched, said I was 'extraordinaire' because the French people hold those songs deep in their memories and hearts, but no one sings them anymore."

After arriving back home in the United States I received a very sweet letter from Merce, appreciating our presence during that delightful week, a week that was apparently stressful for him.

# 34

-:-:-:-:-:-:-:-:-:-:-:-:-:-

## PARIS, NOVEMBER 1999

In 1999, Carolyn, coming from Zurich, and I met in Paris again (no first-class flight this time). We were there to see the company perform, staying, as we had the previous year, in a friend's apartment very near the theater. The combination of being in Paris, visiting with Merce and his company members, and seeing the glorious performances, added up to the feeling that we were dwelling in a small piece of heaven.

This time, the Cunningham company performances were at the former Théâtre Sarah Bernhardt, now the Théâtre de la Ville. We had complimentary tickets for three performances, at all of which *BIPED* would be performed.

During our visit, there was much talk about the internal politics of the company. One significant change was that Merce was less and less involved in the running of the company; he was just focused on his amazing choreography.

November 9: "We saw *Summerspace*, which is a lovely dance, [choreographed in 1958] but Carolyn recognized that the company can't dance that style any more. Carolyn complained about their lack of passion and humanness, which is how things have changed. The Morton Feldman music was lovely, also. However, *BIPED* was astonishing; lush, romantic score a cross between Philip Glass and Prokofiev, very integrated whole: movement, costumes all a-glitter, the remarkable scrim projections—which had less dancers than last summer and more abstraction—I regretted that—gorgeous movements and dancing, and that great music, and wonderful lighting. Very exciting. Many curtain calls—he [Merce] came out—standing straight, but knees all bent out.

"Finally we went downstairs to the reception—jammed, smoke, noise—and Merce had us sit at his little table, and Carolyn said, 'You sit next to him,' which I was happy to do. So we had a lovely chat between admirers. He said, yes, the projections had indeed changed—he liked more dancers, too."

Next performance: "First dance was *Rune*—I thought it was wonderful, and the ensemble work was remarkably 'ensemble.' Tom [Caley] performed very beautifully—crisp and focused and great aerial lightness. Amazing feet—very flexible, almost like Viola's.

"Carolyn said that they don't do it as it was originally done—the style has changed and they are all in the new style. [The two dancers whose faces she felt were expressive were Tom Caley and Holly Farmer.]

"Then *BIPED* again. Such a gorgeous dance. When they are supposed to be in synch they often are not, but it doesn't matter—it's so stunning. The movements are so incredibly original—I can see how the computer releases him. [Merce was using the computer to design movements with the computer bodies which no human body could manage, but which the human body could approximate—and did, quite spectacularly.]

"We joined Alastair Macaulay [then British dance critic, now dance critic for the *New York Times*][1] and David Vaughan and went across the street to Zimmer's for a supper at 10:30 . . . [Zimmer's is a historic nineteenth-century brasserie, with elegant décor from 1896.] Alastair was delightful, amusing, knowledgeable."

Last performance: "We saw *CRWDSPCR*—fantastic robotic dance—I adored it—and enjoyed the interplay between dancers. Lots of couples, ensembles which were 'ensemble'—impressively so. Banu [Ogan] danced well both in this and the next. Holly Farmer and Maydelle Fason have the most 'out' focus and Lisa Boudreau is lovely. Tom [Caley], of course, and a new Japanese man, Koji Minato, look good. Carolyn didn't like it—too robotic for her. I thought it was thrilling. Music was loud—their composer, Takehisa Kosugi, wrote it. But it fit the style. Then *BIPED*—I saw new things this time. It is wonderful and the ending is so dramatic with the slowness and the up and down. I also love all the spinning. I also like Jean Freebury—her dynamic attack and quirkiness. Another reminder of Viola.

"We went backstage after, and I hung out with David and Alastair—finally Trevor [Carlson, Merce's devoted personal assistant][2] called us and we followed him pushing Merce in a wheel chair to his hotel—Orion, I think, at Les Halles. It was a sweet small dinner party with Merce, Alastair, David, Carolyn and me, Trevor and his sister serving us macrobiotic food—lots of it. Merce was relaxed and present, told stories—we all told stories—stayed 'til about 12:30. Merce told stories about his dad, mom, brothers—mom's travels to Alaska, India, flying over Mt. McKinley in a two-seater because she 'won everything' on the cruise. Going back to Cairo to replace a present that had gotten broken in the mails, and telling the shopkeeper, 'I won't ever come back.' His experiences with Mrs. Barrett; telling his parents he wanted to go on stage—his father didn't protest because *he* did what he loved—law. Took him to Cornish School—everyone studied all the arts and concentrated in one—he went in for theatre but took dance with [Martha]

Graham's Bonnie Bird. Cage came in second year, brought 'spirit' to the school, asked him [Merce] to be in his percussion group (all others were teachers) because he had good rhythm and could read music.

"Trevor told me Merce was telling him stories about me—the one about 'the only way to do it is to do it' and the one about 'keeping my hand out but looking away' when collecting money for him. Alastair asked lots of good questions that led to good stories. I told about getting into second position and being unable to jump."

# 35

-:-:-:-:-:-:-:-:-:-:-:-:-:-:-

## PAYING TRIBUTE

Some time in the early 2000s I had a most interesting experience. It confirmed Merce's unique way of teaching movement sequences without imposing any dramatic or emotional content or even using any emotionally laden words. I was attending a company performance and went backstage during the intermission. One of the dancers spotted me and told me she was dancing my part in *Suite for Five* and would appreciate any suggestions I had. She demonstrated one series of movements that I remembered well. Immediately, I told her that when I executed those movements, they had a very romantic feeling. She repeated the movements to include that suggestion. This time the sequence of movements looked just the way I remembered it, and it was very satisfying.

What struck me, as I thought about it, was that I had learned that sequence from Merce simply as a series of leg swings. In performing it as fully and accurately as I could, within the required time frame, what emerged for me was a very romantic experience. Apparently, when we dancers entered fully into the movement sequences we were taught, our bodies responded with an upwelling of emotion. We needed no prompting from the outside to experience that feeling. In my effort to help this young dancer give the movement its fullest expression, however, verbally communicating a feeling was the only way I knew to produce the desired result.

The contrast between the respectful way that Merce taught us his dances, compared to my dependence on imposing emotion to convey the help the young dancer had requested, was a startling experience for me. Yes, my help worked, but what a difference from Merce's trust that the physical body, from within itself, was capable of the most profound and varied expressivity.

April 19, 2009:

Merce's ninetieth birthday celebration occurred during his company's performances at the Brooklyn Academy of Music from April 16–19, 2009. Several friends and associates were invited to make a "toast" to Merce. Three of us accepted. When the time came to make the "toast," the other two said a few words to Merce. I, on the other hand, had carefully composed my homage to Merce on paper with photographs. It was a brief history of his amazing, ground-breaking appearance on the dance scene. I read it with the most drama I could muster, slowly and in full voice. I was standing right in front of Merce, who was sitting in his wheelchair listening, though looking rather tired. There were hundreds of people in the room, all celebrating him and his life and brilliant work. It was a very happy moment for me, to be able to honor him publicly. When I had finished, I gave him the illustrated text and a hug. I believe it was David Vaughan who said he hoped Merce's dancers heard my reading, as they were too young to know any of that history, and it was important for them to know the conventions that he had turned upside down.

Later, I was told that Merce had treasured my "toast."

Here it is:

Once upon a time, a magnificent wild gazelle bounded out of the forest.

As he approached civilization, he assumed human form, without relinquishing his animal grace.

He astounded everyone as he burst upon the stage and danced. Until then, modern dancers had been wedded to the earth, whereas he was totally at home in the air, as well.

-1-

He knew, and demonstrated, that one could be as firmly tethered to the ground on one toe as on two feet, while the rest of one's body was hovering in air.

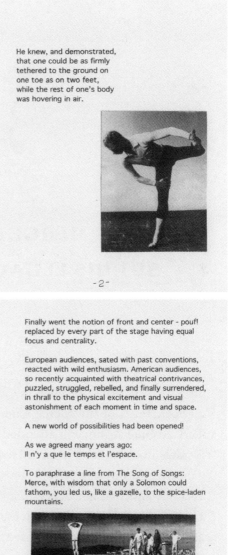

-2-

He began to train his own dancers. He gradually uncoupled them from all conventional supports:

First to go were narrative supports - pouf! replaced by the simple miracle of the human body in motion.

Next went musical supports - pouf! replaced by new sounds occurring in their own context.

Then disappeared the natural flow of movement - pouf! replaced by chance sequences that confounded the intellect while electrifying the body.

The next uncoupling was the habit of continual movement - pouf! now silence and stillness gained equal value.

-3-

Finally went the notion of front and center - pouf! replaced by every part of the stage having equal focus and centrality.

European audiences, sated with past conventions, reacted with wild enthusiasm. American audiences, so recently acquainted with theatrical contrivances, puzzled, struggled, rebelled, and finally surrendered, in thrall to the physical excitement and visual astonishment of each moment in time and space.

A new world of possibilities had been opened!

As we agreed many years ago:
Il n'y a que le temps et l'espace.

To paraphrase a line from The Song of Songs:
Merce, with wisdom that only a Solomon could fathom, you led us, like a gazelle, to the spice-laden mountains.

- 4 -

My presentation to Merce for his ninetieth birthday celebrations, April 2009.

This event was the last time I saw Merce in person.

# 36

-:-:-:-:-:-:-:-:-:-:-:-:-:-:-

## MERCE LEAVES,
## BUT HIS LEGACY IS FOREVER

In 2011, two years after Merce's death, I attended one of the final performances of the Merce Cunningham Dance Company at the Park Avenue Armory.[1] I attended it with my granddaughter, Lizzie Feidelson, who had been interning at the Cunningham Dance Foundation and was living in Brooklyn. (Much to my delight, I had recently watched her dance in a Cunningham Event, performed at the Cunningham studio on Bethune Street in New York City.) She had informed me on the phone the previous day that she had been at a small memorial gathering when Merce's ashes, divided into many small envelopes, had been offered to those present. Members of the Foundation announced that Merce had wanted his ashes tossed into the Hudson River, but that was illegal, so instead, every-one was given a small amount of his ashes, and asked to do some-thing with them to honor Merce.

Lizzie met me downtown in Greenwich Village before the concert, as we had agreed during our phone conversation the day before. She brought her little envelope with her. I decided that we would honor Merce's wish and toss his ashes into the Hudson River. Honor before Law! It was dark already as we hastened across the West Side Highway on a path that permitted safe passage. We realized that since the wind was blowing from the west, it would blow the ashes back at us if we tried to throw them into the river. So instead, we decided to throw the entire little envelope into the river. She handed it to me, and as I threw it as hard and far as I could, I shouted gleefully, "The only way to do it is to do it!"

It felt like the perfect blessing to offer a brilliant, creative, and beloved man, who had blessed my entire life.

# MERCE CUNNINGHAM'S
# DANCE CLASSES

In the late forties and early fifties, Merce would sometimes teach a master class for dance teachers. While waiting for him to enter, they would all sit on the floor, in preparation for the familiar modern dance class opening exercises. He would immediately contradict their expectation: "We're going to start standing on our feet, because that's how we're going to dance." Simple but revolutionary.

Merce's dance classes broke away from standard modern dance practice, particularly Martha Graham's. His class began with everyone standing, rather than sitting. This immediately put attention on an upright spine, strong legs, a sense of balance and an open, outward focus, all of which were important aspects of his choreography.

The opening set of exercises was designed to stretch our bodies in every direction so that we could become flexible in all our parts, including our feet; strengthen our muscles, particularly in our legs; increase our sense of balance; all this while keeping an even rhythm, which in the early days was mostly set by his sharp snapping fingers.

As long as I was there, the first stretches consisted of bending forward toward the floor and lightly bouncing, with our feet in parallel position. Apparently, at some later date, that bouncing was considered harmful to the spine and was eliminated in favor of a steady stretch toward the floor. This exercise was followed by twisting the upper body first to one side, then to the other, always with the feet pointing forward, arms slightly arched by one's side, the head going with the upper torso. We added a small plié while twisting.

Next came attention to legs and feet, extending the legs and feet off the floor in various directions, low then higher, to the front, side, and back, with and without plié, both parallel and then turned out. Thus, we attended to many parts of our bodies in quick succession. There were more stretches that included arm extensions in various arrangements. No part of the body that was in any way movable was ignored. We also practiced moving parts of our bodies slowly, and then moving them rapidly with the same precision (hopefully). And it was all while we were upright on our feet.

His classes also differed from ballet classes, which we attended at the Metropolitan School of Ballet. Ballet classes were also conducted in a standing position, but all the beginning exercises were done at the barre, focused mostly on stretching and extending the legs while practicing the five foot positions (always turned out), the balletic arm movements, and the bending and stretching of the spine. Feet were never parallel. Merce encouraged us to take ballet classes (he never taught ballet classes himself), as the exercises were very helpful in developing strong, flexible, and extended legs and feet. He had studied ballet on arriving in New York from Washington state and knew its value.

The opening exercises were standard practice at every session. It gave Merce an opportunity to watch us and correct us, so that we learned proper alignment, correct hip placement when extending legs, relaxed shoulders during arm movements and properly stretched feet when pointed. A kindly reminder interrupted bad habits (like my tendency to raise my shoulders when learning arm movements).

The middle section of the class put our warmed-up and stretched-out bodies to work dancing. Merce brought choreographed combinations of movements that he demonstrated in class and that we tried to emulate. This demanded an entirely different kind of attention: translating a visual stimulation into a physical response that would hopefully become more and more immediate and intuitive. For some dancers—I think of Carolyn Brown—that translation came easily and quickly, perhaps partly because of her long experience dancing. For other dancers, like me, it was more of a struggle, so I would turn automatically to my well-honed mental activity, trying to "figure it out"—obviously not useful as it only slowed down the learning process. It was this habit that produced Merce's well-known koan: "The only way to do it is to do it." How inscrutable but how right on!

Sometimes his combinations were thrilling to master and execute and I would find myself totally absorbed, moving fully and happily in place or across the floor. Other times, when the combination was difficult for me, I became a worker (or as I labeled it in my journal, an "athlete," which I had been in my childhood) rather than a dancer. That was not fun.

These combinations became more complex as we became more adept at learning them. Often they were actually small parts of a dance that he was choreographing. As time went on, and we began learning dances and performing them, these might be an opportunity for him to see what a series of movements looked like on his dancers, and how the dancers could perform them. We never knew whether these practice pieces were just for class or for a larger project, until we might see them appear when we were learning a new dance.

In this section of the class, Merce would deliberately let us find our own way of replicating his combinations. He never imposed a particular style. This allowed our individual way of moving to emerge and gave Merce an opportunity to observe what that was.

For those of us who became company members, his observations facilitated Merce's ability to exploit our particular styles in designing his choreography. He made wonderful use of Carolyn's purity, clarity, and precision of movement in all his elegant solos and duets for her; Viola's awkwardness and uninhibited expressiveness contributed an alternative set of possibilities for his creative juices; Remy brought strength, flexibility, comfort in the air; I had strong legs for going up in the air and down to the floor. JoAnn Melsher, while she was with the company, had wonderful bounce and energy, which he put to excellent use when choreographing *Banjo*, in which she had the original lead role, given to Carolyn when JoAnn left the company.

The closing exercise of the class was jumping in place with our legs together and apart. Although I have no clear memory of the difference between the class he taught in Paris in the summer of 1949 and the class he started in New York upon arriving home, the fact that I got stymied in the final jumping assignment in my first class in New York suggests the possibility that those final jumps were not part of the Paris class. In all likelihood, he was continually developing his class structure.

Merce's own physical gifts set a superb example for his students. His body was as mercurial as his nature: he was splendid when upright, when in the air, and when down on the floor. He was as flexible as a rubber band, and very strong. He choreographed incredibly distorted and complex movements for some of his solos, using chance operations, but he never let their difficulty stop him from carrying them out to perfection. This was the body we observed in motion in class; inspiring, if a bit intimidating.

# AFTERWORD

## I

Paris! The events related by this memoir begin chronologically in that city in 1949. For fifty years, many Americans had looked on the French capital city as the epicenter of modernity in the arts. Paris had been home to the French artists who had composed *La Mer* (Debussy), had painted *La Danse* (Matisse), had written and directed *Le Sang d'un poète* (Cocteau), had written *L'Étranger* (Camus) and *Antigone* (Anouilh); Paris was where non-French artists had come to make their most important work: *Les Demoiselles d'Avignon* (Picasso), *Le Sacre du printemps* (Stravinsky), *Ulysses* (Joyce), *The Sun Also Rises* (Hemingway), and many more. Isadora Duncan had lived, loved, danced, and grieved in Paris; Gertrude Stein had written breakthrough modernist work and been a patron to artists of several genres there; *Le Sacre* was just one of the many sensational premieres given there by Diaghilev's Ballets Russes.

After the Second World War, however, Paris reminded many of its American visitors that they had left a younger such epicenter behind them: New York. As a result of the disruptions of European politics, many Old World artists had moved to the New World.

Even when peace returned to Europe, many of them remained in America.

Marianne Preger (as she was then) was—and is—one of life's enthusiasts. She did not make invidious comparisons between countries or cities; she loved Paris. Yet, though she came to Paris to study French theater, her visit's big epiphany came when she saw the American dancer who is her main subject here: Merce Cunningham. She had already admired him a few years before, when he was performing with the Martha Graham Dance Company. Now, performing his own choreography, he had arrived in his element, at age thirty. Marianne Preger committed herself, there and then, to his work. Later that year, they returned to New York at more or less the same time. She became his first student.

The years that followed brought her into contact with John Cage and Robert Rauschenberg. Like Cunningham, these now-famous figures weren't famous then. And the dancers weren't paid; Preger and her colleagues took other jobs to subsidize their dance habit. In 1953, the Merce Cunningham Dance Company was formed, at Black Mountain College, with her among its founding members; but Preger scarcely noticed—work just carried on much as before. Who guessed then that Cunningham's teaching and choreography would become internationally renowned, and would remain so after his death? Preger was part of his first New York season (at the Theatre de Lys—now the Lucille Lortel) and his first seriously successful tour (the American West Coast, 1955). Among the roles she created for Cunningham were in two of his most lastingly important works: *Septet* (1953) and *Suite for Five* (1955). These dances are still performed; so are excerpts from other pieces in whose original casts she appeared: *Dime-a-Dance* (1953), *Minutiae* (1954), and *Springweather and People* (1955).

Marianne Preger is sunny, warm, a naturally positive thinker. Cunningham—though capable of humor, high energy, feral intensity, and enthusiasm—was often guarded, indirect, moody, and, outside his own dance concerns, a poor communicator. Often, he found himself developing a friendship with one particular member of the company—usually female, and often the least psychologically needy one. Preger became the prototype of these. Other dancers doubted Cunningham's affection for them; she never did.

In her final seasons, newly married, she danced as Marianne Simon. When she left, in 1958, it was with reluctance—and with joy at the prospect of starting a family. And so she was not a part of the Cunningham company's biggest successes, which occurred between the mid-1960s and 2011, in New York, around the United States, and in many other countries. News of them brought her only delight. Over the years, Cunningham and she kept in touch. When her chosen duties as wife, mother (two children), teacher, and—later—psychotherapist permitted, she came to watch his company.

With wonderful symmetry, she returned to Paris in 1998 and 1999 to watch the Cunningham troupe in two of its most clamorously acclaimed seasons. She traveled with Carolyn Brown, who had become Cunningham's most eminent co-dancer between 1953 and 1972, and with whom she had remained friends. On those visits to Paris, she had no intention of writing this memoir—yet those seasons give her Cunningham memories a fifty-year arc. Cunningham had been the Nijinsky of modern dance when she saw him there in 1949, the foremost figure in his own choreography, a dancer of phenomenal elevation and animal intensity. Now almost all his creations were for far younger performers; many of the final Cunningham audiences never saw Cunningham dance.

It was during the 1999 Paris season that I was introduced to Preger. She and I both recall a number of meals before or after performance when she, Brown, David Vaughan, and I all conversed merrily. I was the new boy; those three had all known one another since the 1950s. Vaughan had written about Cunningham for decades, was the company's archivist, and had recently published the first edition of his definitive *Merce Cunningham: Fifty Years*. (In 2012, it appeared in an enlarged and brilliantly illustrated iPad edition as *Merce Cunningham: 65 Years*, now available on the Merce Cunningham Trust website.) Brown was gradually preparing the memoir that, in 2007, came out as *Chance and Circumstance: Twenty Years with Cage and Cunningham*. I, having written reviews of Cunningham since 1979, had recently begun work on another Cunningham book (still incomplete). Only now do we look back on those happy dinners as ones for four Cunningham writers, but that's another of this book's satisfying symmetries.

Preger, Brown, Vaughan, and I all found it easy to share our different responses to Cunningham's latest work. That was the first season his *BIPED*—a sensational magnum opus, new that year—was seen in Paris; we all knew it took Cunningham's work in new directions, lifting the final, "computer" phase of his choreography to new levels of dramatic poetry. Since 1989, Cunningham had been using a dance computer as a compositional tool; his first work created with its assistance had reached the stage in 1991. To hear Preger and Brown voice their great admiration for Cunningham's new work, decades after they had danced for him, was moving. They knew that Cunningham was now lame; they related tenderly how, back in the day, he had demonstrated every move he made for them, and they marveled at how he had elicited new qualities of motion from his young performers. There was, as Preger relates here, one dinner at which we, at his request, joined him; I remember that you could feel the warmth between Preger and him, like a glow in the air.

Brown and Preger were friends from the year they met, 1953. They were unalike, and they viewed Cunningham differently—but, then and later, they made their divergences part of a continuing conversation. Brown was married to one of Cunningham's composers, Earle Brown; Preger was the daughter of a psychiatrist. Brown's book, while it shows a profound and detailed understanding of the artistic dimensions of Cunningham's work, frequently shows how often she was severe on him and hurt by him. Preger, though touchingly aware of his dark moods, writes with broader shoulders and a broader understanding of his personality. And one of this memoir's many endearing features is the way it reveals these two women were having those conversations about him back then. They admired each other; Brown begins her memoir by recalling how, when she retired, she wanted to do so with the good grace that Preger had shown:

> Most of all, I wanted to leave "well." Only one of Merce's dancers had managed that in the past: Marianne Preger. With grace and good humor and abundant love, she managed to depart the company, having chosen motherhood and family after more than eight years dancing with Merce. Without feeling rejected, Merce was able to accept her decision. Like Marianne, I wanted to leave without ill feeling, rancor, or bitterness.[1]

## II

In a 1949 *Dance Observer* essay called "An American in Paris," Cunningham, too, wrote about his recent period in that city. He had spent six months in the Netherlands and Italy, but mainly in France. One terse line was simply, "Europe is fascinating, but not essential." He went on:

> Paris is a wonderful city, pleasant to see, to live in, and to enjoy. The food is splendid, the parks are like being in the country, the museums, all that is superb. But I've seen no dancing that even touches what takes place in the United States. Dancing here is divertissement, a spectacle to be looked at and if it's accompanied by enough sets and costumes maybe it will cause a furore.... [2]

About teaching modern dance in Paris, he observed:

> The French attack on time is very peculiar. If a class runs from 6.30 to 7.30 they feel it's possible to arrive at any point within that hour and start the class. At least it keeps bringing in new faces.

And French choreography prompted him to write this:

> Les Ballets de Paris of Roland Petit is comparable to our
> musical comedies, not as slickly done, and on the whole our
> musicals have better dancers. Their ballets are more entertain-
> ing than our musicals, because the ballets don't pretend to
> be serious, but Agnes de Mille and Jerry Robbins are much
> better choreographers than Petit.

Cunningham had grown up in Washington state; he always said that, on his 1939 arrival in New York, he had stepped onto the sidewalk, looked at the skyline, and said, "This is home." From then on, he lived in New York. Seventy years later, he died there, in 2009. When he and Cage returned to America in 1949, they knew it was where they belonged. Cunningham especially: Cage loved to spend time far from the madding crowd, but Cunningham relished city life, New York's above all.

Even so, Paris was good to Cage and Cunningham. Cage collected scores by his favorite composer, Erik Satie; Cunningham explored lesser-known areas of French literature; and they both mixed with a wide range of visual artists. The 1949 dances Cunningham made there for himself with Tanaquil Le Clercq (the duet *Amores*) and also Betty Nichols (the trio *Effusions avant l'heure*) were seen by distinguished audiences, including Alice B. Toklas and Alberto Giacometti. Cunningham always loved to relate how Toklas, having told him she enjoyed his work, asked him to ask her why. So he did. She answered, emphatically, "Because it was so pagan." (Cunningham would relate this with high amusement.) He was pleased enough with those dances to show them in his next New York performance, at Hunter College, in January 1950. (Curiously, although the title *Effusions avant l'heure* was a paraphrase of its music's title, *A Valentine Out of Season*, he now changed its name to *Games*.) *Amores* remained in his repertory for several years, with Brown succeeding Le Clercq as his partner. He also spent his Paris summer preparing other dances for that 1950 New York concert.

Decades later, Paris became the scene for his greatest accolades and audience ovations. In 1964, the theater director Peter Brook attended a Cunningham performance in Paris. He then wrote a foreword for Cunningham's first London season that year, including these words:

> Merce Cunningham's work is of the highest quality and of great importance. It searches in new directions, it is free, it is open to the play of all the forces which the artists involved sense without being able to control—and yet it is precise, classical and severe.

It was in Paris, in the first Cunningham season at the Théâtre de la Ville, in 1972, that Brown gave her final performance. That ended one era—but began another, as the Théâtre de la Ville then became the company's main French home until 2011. (It also danced for several seasons at the Paris Opéra and the courtyard of the Palais Royal. A number of important Cunningham works had their premieres in one Parisian theater or another.) After one 1996 Théâtre de la Ville performance of *Sounddance* (1975), the applause was so intense that the usually contained Cunningham blew kisses to the audience. (That was wholly uncharacteristic of him; Brown did not quite believe it when I told her.) It remains moving that Preger and Brown, important parts of Cunningham's history, were there to witness these important Paris seasons.

### III

It's impressive that, when Preger experienced the life-changing revelation of Cunningham's dancing and choreography in 1949, she was a drama student. His work has often been described as if it was "just" pure dance, more theory than emotion—the same is still sometimes said of the less radical George Balanchine in ballet. Nonetheless, dance for Cunningham was always a form of theater. Ellen Cornfield, who danced with Cunningham in the years

1974–1983, once said, "I believe Merce is very emotional, and his choreography is his way of handling that emotion." Many of his dancers would agree; and all of them experienced his effort to make his dances register theatrically.

When he went to study at the Cornish School in Seattle, in 1937, aged eighteen, his main subject was not dance but theater. He tried to pursue both disciplines—he had been dancing since childhood—but evidence suggests that theater would have remained his chief area had he not clashed with Alexander Koriansky, the conservative head of the Cornish theater department. Koriansky had no interest in "the new"; Bonnie Bird, the new head of the Cornish dance department and a former dancer in Martha Graham's dance company, had plenty. No choreographer at that time better demonstrated than Graham how dance could be a new form of theater; Cunningham, thanks to his modern-dance studies with Bird, joined Graham's troupe in 1939. While living in New York in the early 1940s, he performed in a few modern plays; and Graham gave him a speaking role in the 1942 performances of her *American Document* (1937) and in the 1943 premiere of her *Salem Shore*. His own early work *Four Walls* (1944) included an extensive script, written by him along modernist lines related to Gertrude Stein, James Joyce, and others.

Over the decades, Cunningham dance theater came to exemplify radical new directions in drama. In the 1960s, he was admired not just by Peter Brook but by a generation of advanced directors at London's Royal Court (Lindsay Anderson and William Gaskill went to his performances for the rest of their lives). The independence of music, dance, and design—a central feature of Cunningham dance theater, developed in the years while Preger danced for him—made one dramatic impact after another in successive works; it connected to, and often went beyond, the achievements of what was then called the Theatre of the Absurd (Samuel Beckett, Eugene Ionesco, Harold Pinter).

Each Cunningham work, very evidently, created its own world.

Often the most talked-of feature of each was its music or its design—but there was no doubt that the individual style of each piece came in its movement. One work would have striking quantities of stillness (Preger remembers these especially in *Springweather and People*); another was all nonstop movement; one seemed about wildlife; another full of tension and violence; another was Zen-like in its emphasis on movement that was about itself, without any imagery suggesting anything else. Movement became dramatic by way of its sheer rigor.

For Cunningham and colleagues, some of the thought behind this came from reading Antonin Artaud. Artaud, who advocated the so-called Theatre of Cruelty and admired Balinese and other Southeast Asian forms of theater for their ways of taking drama away from the tyranny of text, had died in 1948. His best-known work, *Le Théâtre et son double* (1938), had never been translated until Mary Caroline (always known as "M.C.") Richards—poet, potter, and close member of Cunningham's artistic circle—did so. It was published in 1958 as *The Theatre and Its Double*; Preger writes here how she helped with that translation.

The wordless theater that Cunningham devised in the 1950s was game-changing in many ways. He had devised a new dance technique that endures as one of the foremost training disciplines in world dance. He was developing a form of dance theater where the dancers often discovered what they were going to wear for each work around the time of the dress rehearsal and where they only heard the music at the premiere. And the music was often composed with elements of indeterminacy that made it unpredictable during each performance. Would music, design, and dance unite in harmony in performance or would they clash? Both options were theatrically valid for Cunningham: décor and music were environments but, sometimes, arrestingly hostile ones.

People often asked (and still ask) "What's this work of art about?" In dance, nobody went further than he in making the question irrelevant—or deeply ambiguous. John Updike, writing about the 1950s, once listed "their emphasis upon private space, their disdainful regard for public concerns, their sense of hermetic, disengaged artistry, and their New Criticism faith that all essential information is contained within the work itself." ("Nabokov's Lectures," *Hugging the Shore: Essays and Criticism by John Updike*, Penguin, UK, 1985, p. 235) Though Updike was not talking about Cunningham's choreography, he might as well have been. With each Cunningham dance, its audience entered a new world. To some, those zones still seem arcane, cold—but to many, they take the drama of dance theater as far as it has ever gone.

## IV

Who knows, when things are happening, what significances will emerge with hindsight? Today, Cage and Cunningham are sometimes extolled as one of the great gay couples of artistic history. They became an item, we now know, in 1943, and for fifty years—1942–92—they made music and choreography together. Yet they kept their sexuality a private matter until 1989; Preger writes here how she was unaware of it until long after her departure from the company. (Vaughan, who knew them both from the mid-1950s, did not realize they were a couple until he was booking the rooms for the company's 1964 world tour. Cage and Cunningham did not share a New York apartment until the 1970s.) Both Preger and Brown have written how all the company's women dancers were somewhat in love with Cunningham; the way in which Preger writes of this is full of affection and respect.

When the Cunningham company reached its fiftieth anniversary in 2003, that was treated as a milestone for celebration. So it's amusing here to read that its formation scarcely registered on Preger. She was already dancing for Cunningham before then; nothing much seemed to change. The time the company spent at Black Mountain College, that arena of avant-garde experimentation, registered as another prolonged tour stop, but little more. (One of its two revelations for her came with yogurt and black molasses. Well, the yogurt, at any rate.)

But Preger certainly registers here the importance of Cunningham's 1954 season at New York's Theatre de Lys, as she does with the company's three-week 1955 tour of the American West Coast. After its appearance in San Francisco, she wrote to her parents, "And do you know, Margot Fonteyn did 'Swan Lake' the same night and we got all the critics!" (She also mentions a television appearance the company made in Portland, Oregon. If ever video of this screening were to emerge, it would be one of the earliest records of the company's work. Alas, it seems to have been lost.)

Another 1955 trip took the company to Jacob's Pillow. Today, that famous, rural dance institution in inland Massachusetts maintains one of the world's most remarkable dance archives, in which you can see silent footage of that Cunningham 1955 season—far briefer than we would like but welcome nonetheless. These include Preger and Brown dancing with Cunningham in his *Banjo* and *Septet*.

Fifty-four years later, Preger and Brown were there again for the opening night of the Cunningham company's season. That night, a Wednesday, is the starting-point of Marianne's memoir (another of its touching symmetries). It was widely known that Cunningham was close to death that week, at his home in New York; he died some hours after the final Pillow performance on Sunday. But he watched that Wednesday performance in a live-stream relay. Before it, as Preger relates, she and Brown were invited to speak to him. It's characteristic of their friendship that she began the conversation with humor, laughingly reminding him of an old mishap during the company's 1955 season there.

Amid the mirth they all shared in her dancing days, Preger also recalls serious conversations with Cunningham and Cage, often while crossing the country on other tours. In diary entries, written then and quoted here, she vividly records Cunningham's words on the evolution and purpose of the dance technique he taught, and Cage's on the value of Zen philosophy.

# V

During his lifetime, few people saw any of Cunningham's choreographic notes. In his late years, assistants were allowed to consult these for specific older works when restaging them. Today, however, the originals are in the New York Public Library for the Performing Arts. (Copies are kept by the Cunningham Trust.) They do not solve the mysteries of his work; but they deepen its fascination. Today, the notes for *Septet* (1953) and *Springweather and People* (1955) bring revelations.

*Septet* has been performed by a number of companies over the decades. It's the only surviving work in which anyone can see and hear how Cunningham's choreography fits the rhythms and structures of its score, in this case Erik Satie's suite for piano duet *Trois morceaux en forme de poire*. The name *Septet* comes from its number not of dancers (six) but of musical sections (seven). Cunningham said its creation was one of the last times he followed a wholly intuitive process. Brown, Preger, and Viola Farber were its original three women; Brown danced a remarkable duet with Cunningham, which ended with Cunningham lifting her and carrying her tenderly offstage while she framed his face with one arm. Brown writes, "What a joy to be learning a part made directly on me, for the dancer I was then, the dancer he saw in me, rather than learning a role made on someone else." The fragmentary Jacob's Pillow 1955 films show Cunningham, Brown, and Preger (Farber's role at that performance was taken by Anita Dencks). In 1963, a beautiful film was made of the complete work, with the score played with terrific force by Cage and Tudor (parts can be seen on YouTube); Cunningham, Brown, and Farber are among the dancers, and Brown's great beauty and distinction burn in the memory.

One *Septet* mystery has long been discussed. A dance for Cunningham and the three women makes an unmistakable reference to a closing section from Balanchine's ballet *Apollo* (1928), given an altered, freeze-frame emphasis. It's possible to see echoes of several choreographers (Petipa, Nijinsky, Graham, Astaire, Balanchine) in various Cunningham dances, but here is the one example where Cunningham seems, emphatically, to be drawing his source to his audience's attention. Yet when David Vaughan asked Cunningham about this *Apollo* reference, Cunningham insisted that he was thinking there of the Indian legend of Krishna and the gopis. (Probably he was thinking of both.)

Neither *Apollo* nor Krishna feature in any of Cunningham's sets of notes for *Septet*. These exist in three main sets, and their first revelation is that, though *Septet* had its premiere in 1953, the notes he made for that premiere are not his first. He had, it emerges, planned large parts of a detailed earlier version, probably in 1952; this *Septet* was to have had not six dancers but ten or eleven. He was to have the lead role; Preger was to be part of the cast. Brown, however, was not yet in Cunningham's sights. The work's central duet was planned, move by move, for himself and Joan Skinner (by all accounts a beautifully distinguished dancer, from the Graham company, remembered by Preger and Brown; she later gained another distinction as the inventor of Skinner Release Technique). Cunningham's notes for this duet conclude "M. carries J. off after music is finished," one of many signs that this duet—never realized in rehearsal or onstage—was close to the one he later staged with Brown in 1953. The 1952 notes, however, show that Cunningham planned the duet to be in the foreground, offset by a background group dance; the latter was never realized. Diagrams for a subsequent quartet for Cunningham and three women are very close to the 1953 version (and very close to the still unmentioned *Apollo*).

More surprising is that his initial notes for this first draft of *Septet*, accompanied by a 1903 edition of the Satie score, refer to the novels of Pierre Louÿs (1870–1925)—once a best-selling author in French, but little known in English. A friend of Oscar Wilde, André Gide, and Claude Debussy (Wilde dedicated the first French edition of

*Salomé* to him), Louÿs wrote erotic poems and fiction that evoke the world or worlds of ancient Greek history and mythology. They're remarkable not least for their attention to female sexuality and frankness about lesbian themes. His prose-poems *Chansons de Bilitis* (1894) inspired Debussy to a song-cycle (of the same name, 1897–98) and to the piano pieces *Antique Epigraphs* (1914); his novel *Aphrodite: moeurs antiques* (*Aphrodite: ancient morals*, 1896), set in ancient Alexandria, concerns a young courtesan of much-admired beauty, Chrysis, and a sculptor, Demétrios, amid a story that includes lesbians and a temple of Aphrodite/Astarte that houses fourteen hundred courtesans. Chrysis, perversely, demands that the sculptor give her three objects that can only be won by crimes (theft, murder, sacrilege). His love and hers travel in different directions: she commits suicide by hemlock, whereupon he uses her dead nude body as a model as he creates the statue of Immortal Life. An early note of Cunningham reads "Tanagra; greek; world of Louÿs; Alexandria; Chrysis; Aphrodite." For one section, he writes *"Preparations for a funeral* Flowers, black robes, candles placed here & there. Individuals run on & off. With different things; others run on & change preceding things & run off." Several of his notes are in French; they refer as much or more to Louÿs than to Satie: "tristesse profonde," "indolence de rythme (Manière de commencement-en plus)." "gaieté joviale (no 2)," "mélancolie souriante (redite)." Nonetheless, any connections between Louÿs and the dance notes here are, at best, oblique. *Aphrodite* is certainly a most surprising book for Cunningham to have known. Onstage he tended to avoid same-sex couplings; and no sexual implications in his work were remotely as overt as they are in Louÿs.

Reading these notes in 2016, I immediately wrote to Preger (who was characteristically encouraging), Brown, and Vaughan. They helped me identify the dancers Cunningham named solely by first names—but they confirmed they had never heard of this earlier sketch. Nor had Louÿs ever been mentioned, in 1953 or later. I already knew from other Cunningham notes that such puzzles and surprises abound in them. His work had long shown that his mind was remarkably multilayered, but his notes reveal more layers yet.

When he created *Septet* in 1953 on its first actual cast—at Black Mountain College—they loved learning and performing it. They all felt it had dramas and meanings, even if he wasn't telling. Two years after its premiere, however, without informing them, he wrote a program note, saying "The poetic ambiguity of the music and dance titles express the character of the ballet, whose subject is Eros, and whose occurrence is the intersection of joy and sorrow." He also now supplied titles to each section: "In the Garden," "In the Music Hall," "In the Tea House," "In the Playground," "In the Morgue," "In the Distance," and "In the End." Decades later, David Vaughan asked Cunningham where these titles came from. Cunningham replied, "They're from me." The titles did not necessarily reflect their content, he said; he'd invented them for rehearsal purposes. In *Chance and Circumstance*, Carolyn Brown remembers speculating in 1953 that Cunningham's "intersection of joy and sorrow" came from something in his own past (p. 67). She also remembers hearing that "For 'In the Morgue' (or 'the couple dance' as we called it), Merce is said to have wanted candelabra as décor" (p. 69), though he never told her this himself; she was therefore gratified in 2016 to read of the "Preparations for a funeral" note in his pre-1953 notes. My own guess is that "Eros" as subject, the "intersection of joy and sorrow," and the funeral idea were all prompted by ideas in Louÿs's *Aphrodite*.

We'll never know now for sure, however. The mysteries of Merce Cunningham tend to increase rather than diminish. And does it matter where the ideas came from? For many artists of his day, the "subject" of a work was simply an igniting spark. The painter Willem de Kooning, with whom Cunningham had crossed paths in New York and Black Mountain, later said, "Content, if you want to say, is a glimpse of something, an encounter, you know, like a flash—it's very tiny, very tiny, content."[3] Cunningham's notes all suggest that this was true for him, too. Sometimes, even in later compositions of the 1970s and 1980s, he begins them with a literary or expressive idea, but that's simply something to get him going. As he builds the dance, he almost never needs to return to the generating concept.

Here and in many works, Cunningham exemplifies the points made by Susan Sontag in her great essay "Against Interpretation" (1966), which quotes that line by de Kooning. Indeed, Sontag refers to Cunningham as an exemplary artist, before reaching her conclusion:

> Our task is not to find the maximum amount of content in a work of art, much less to squeeze more content out of the work than is already there. Our task is to cut back content so that we can see the thing at all.
>
> The aim of all commentary on art now should be to make works of art—and, by analogy, our own experience—more, rather than less, real to us. The function of criticism should be to show how it is what it is, even that it is what it is, rather than to show what it means.
>
> In place of a hermeneutics we need an erotics of art.[4]

Yet, even after his death, Cunningham can spring further surprises. Another notebook of his, containing further *Septet* notes, dates from 1973. Usually, when Cunningham returns to old choreography, it's just to attend to its facts. Here, however, he seems to be trying to see if *Septet* will still work. He and Brown had performed it often until 1964; then he'd let it lapse from repertory. Now, the year after Brown's departure from the company, he revisits his twenty-year-old creation—and does so in terms of meaning.

He draws attention to the intimacies of the duet ("close positions; lifts with intimate actions—face on cheek; hand on breast; hand in hand") and mentions amid section "4" ("Playground") a "change of characters from 3 girls to 1 girl & 2 men—'sex introduction'; fast lift carried through space; flash exit." He still calls section "5" a "Funeral preparation in silence ahead of music; people taking their places in formal behavior (what does that idea equate with now?) (Young people—Woodstock—no, 60s)."

Joan Skinner and other points of his original notes are forgotten in Cunningham's 1970s notes on *Septet*; he refers to Brown's role and his as "CB" and "MC." But what's uncharacteristic is the way Cunningham, returning to his old work, starts to interpret it. Who'd have thought he'd see one trio as a sex introduction? Who imagined that he would see another sequence in terms of Woodstock and the 1960s?

## VI

Preger and Brown were also in the original cast for *Springweather and People* (1955). For years, this was one of Cunningham's lost works. It has some historical importance, since it was the first of a series of four works about the seasons; there followed *Summerspace* (1958), *Rune* (1960—originally planned as *Autumn Rune*), and *Winterbranch* (1964). Those later three works all kept returning to repertory in subsequent decades, but *Springweather* was dropped before he even made *Summerspace*. Its memory, however, was cherished. Preger remembered its exceptional use of stillness; Brown, though she did not recall that, spoke of its marvelous lyricism.

In 2015, however, the researcher and filmmaker Alla Kovgan found a German TV film of Cunningham and Brown dancing, among other items, their duet from *Springweather*. And in 2016 I began to examine Cunningham's notes for it; I may have been the second person after Cunningham himself ever to do so. Both Brown and Preger were right: the duet (which has now been reconstructed and danced by several groups, including the L.A. Dance Project) is a marvel of lyricism, beautifully and suspensefully danced, while the notes show that stillness was a crucial concern of Cunningham's.

The notes are bewildering; there are hundreds of handwritten pages in three folders, whose original order is often hard to determine, but they are among the first to demonstrate how Cunningham—shaking dice—used chance.

One page says:

Throw for structure <1 + 1 + 36 + 38 & on>
—throw for number of people using same structure
—throw for moving & stillness
—throw for moving & stillness
—throw for sticking to minute division of structure
—throw for new entrances in middle of structure
throw for length of phrasing (i.e. 1, 2 as more structures)

Another page has:

2 heads—1 3
1 head & 1 tail—13
2 tails—12
heads—all same (slow or fast)
heads—slow movement
head & tail—medium
tails—fast

Cunningham determined in advance what chance should determine: the structure of space and time, the choice of dance units (duets, solos, trios, and so on), which parts of the body, which combinations of stillness and movement. The structure of the whole piece emerges as an elaborate study in Cagean "square-root" form. (John Cage, in his early search for an overall rhythmic structure, often used a format he had admired in one piece by Satie, organizing a piece in terms, say, of 12 × 12 or 17 × 17.) Cunningham would revert to this method in later years: one of the marvelous solos for *Doubles* was planned as 13 × 13, another 14 × 14, and so on); but the whole of *Springweather*, while it includes individual 9 × 9 sections, is planned as a single structure of 38 × 38. (Each 38 is subdivided: 13 + 13 + 12.) To an outsider who never saw *Springweather*, these mathematical constructions—within which chance operations were used to make so many specific choices—are mind-boggling. But they're just as bewildering to those who were part of *Springweather*. Preger and Brown have confirmed that all this arithmetic was never mentioned to them.

But as the *Springweather* notes develop, certain imagery starts to recur: "tempest" and "idyll" are recurrent words. Another key word is "silence," which may well refer to Cage's 4'33", the famous, or notorious, three-part musical composition, completed in 1952, in which the player played no music. Probably the "silence" of these notes became the "motionlessness" remembered by Preger (though Cunningham in several dances sometimes cleared the stage of all dancers for lengths of time). But two other operative terms here are "neutral" and "phrase." And another reiterated adjective is "still-moving," an oxymoron which may mean (as in several other Cunningham dances) that one part of the body moved while another part remained still. Of course, I asked Preger and Brown in 2016 if Cunningham had ever used those words in rehearsing *Springweather*. Of course, the answer was "No."

Cunningham was a man of secrets; and he seems never to have told anyone just how he prepared a dance. "My mind always turns toward complexity," he would say with a rueful smile. Those reports of his dark moods shouldn't surprise us today. When we start to see just how intricate his dances were before he ever taught them to the dancers, we realize what huge powers of concentration he required of himself.

The most extensive study of Cunningham's notes to date has been made by Patricia Lent, who danced in his company in 1984–1993 and is now the Cunningham Trust's director of licensing. Concentrating on the dances made in the era she was with the company, she consistently observes that Cunningham's notes, even at their most precise, did not function like a score in music. He worked from them while creating the dance, but, as his choreography turned from text into three-dimensional life before him, he was happy to make adjustments. (Always he delighted in the realities the dancers showed him, which often inspired him.) Lent:

> As a new dancer . . . I learned that Merce was deeply interested and remarkably tolerant of the way different dancers saw, learned, and danced his movement. It was not about being right or wrong, it was about an authentic collaborative process, one that brought together, in the studio, Merce's plans and intentions, often worked out months in advance, and the actions of a particular group of dancers at a particular time.[5]

You couldn't reconstruct *Springweather* from these old notes, almost all of which were made before rehearsals began. As Brown relates in *Chance and Circumstance*, the dancer JoAnn Melsher suddenly withdrew from the company during rehearsals, so that the whole piece had to be reorganized at short notice with one fewer performer.

Cunningham was a realist. Neither with *Springweather* nor any of his later works did he try later on to return to the original choreography he had planned on the page: the actual dance, as it found its form around the time of the premiere, was what mattered. In the classroom, teaching Preger a seemingly impossible step, he had made her laugh by saying, "Marianne, the only way to do it is to do it." He could have applied the same motto in the making of his dances.

## VII

Preger and Brown had fun making up stories for the dances Cunningham gave them. Preger, however, seems always to have been content not to know what original ideas were in Cunningham's mind. Along the way, she learnt something else that mattered more to her: that a work develops its own inner feeling for the executant.

*Suite for Five*, she knew, was and is one of the ultimate examples of dance that's about nothing but itself—yet she also remembered how it felt to do. She relates here how, in the early 2000s, a younger dancer consulted her about the role she had created; she, some forty-seven years after the premiere, passed on how one movement had felt "romantic." This made just the right difference to its execution. But what's most touching about Preger's way of telling this story is that she separates that romantic feeling from Cunningham's intention, and, after so many decades, keeps on understanding Cunningham yet better:

> The contrast between the respectful way that Merce taught us his dances, compared to my dependence on imposing emotion to convey the help the young dancer had requested, was a startling experience for me. Yes, my help worked, but what a difference from Merce's trust that the physical body, from within itself, was capable of the most profound and varied expressivity.[6]

Many dancers find that they understand better in retrospect what they had been part of. Few write with Preger's blend of sensitivity and generosity. Throughout these pages, she's good company—and she makes you love the company she kept. She was in Merce Cunningham's orbit. Here she counts her blessings.

*Alastair Macaulay*
*New York, October 2017*

# ACKNOWLEDGMENTS

I am grateful to so many people who have assisted me in the writing and publication of this book. I want to mention them in chrono-logical order, because it starts way back in time:

My college and forever friend, Alta Ann Morris, was generous and wise enough to send me all the letters I wrote to her when I was in Paris, which allowed this book to exist; my parents were thought-ful enough to do the same.

My husband, Tom Leamon, a gifted writer himself, edited the original text and most important, taught me how to untangle sen-tences that were tripping over clauses (I call him Santa Claus).

Carolyn Brown was the next person who read and edited an early version of the text and in addition to expressing great enthusiasm for my efforts, suggested removing about two dozen exclamation points, thank goodness.

Next was David Vaughan, archivist for the Cunningham com-pany, to whom I sent a version minus exclamation points—he also expressed warm enthusiasm and encouragement, along with urging me to make the book longer.

With considerable trepidation, I finally sent the text to Alastair Macaulay, senior dance critic for the *New York Times*, whom I had met and knew was a great fan of Merce Cunningham. He also expressed vigorous enthusiasm and spent many months and years asking me questions in a marvelously successful attempt to pull more information from my brain, as the book slowly grew in size and depth. I owe him an incredible debt of gratitude for the time, patience, and brilliance that inch by inch produced a reasonably sized book; as well as for taking the initiative to finally submit the text to the University Press of Florida, along with a wonderful afterword, and an offer to caption my illustrations, for which I am profoundly grateful.

Because of that move, I landed in the remarkably competent, patient, encouraging, and devoted hands of their editor, Mindy Aloff, who has elicited even more writing from me and expressed enthusiasm for every bit of it as it appeared on her computer screen in the middle of the night.

Finally, I owe deep appreciation to my friend and neighbor, Marie-Hélène Huet, a French professor and experienced writer. She encouraged, and edited, more descriptions, details, and information about my experiences enjoying famous artists of all kinds in postwar France.

I must add lengthy applause and cheers for the geniuses who devised the computer. I can't imagine doing all this revision on a typewriter.

# NOTES

### Chapter 1. At the End

1. From "Scones," a poem by Gelia Dolcimascolo, in *Heart By Heart: Mothers and Daughters Listening to Each Other*, Marianne Preger-Simon, iUniverse, 2004.

### Chapter 8. One Step Leads to Another

1. *Effusions Avant l'Heure*, renamed *Games* in 1950, and then *Trio* in 1953, when I danced in it. Cunningham later danced *Amores* with Carolyn Brown.

### Chapter 11. Dancing

1. Dance Critics Panel, "The Forming of an Aesthetic: Merce Cunningham and John Cage" (part of the Dance Critics Association Conference of June 16, 1984, held at The Kitchen, in New York City), *Ballet Review* 13:3 (fall 1985).
2. State University of New York Festival panel, titled "Cunningham and His Dancers," March 1987, *Ballet Review* 15:3 (fall 1987).

### Chapter 16. Zen and the Art of Music

1. Lewis Hyde, *Trickster Makes This World: Mischief, Myth and Art* (New York: Farrar, Straus and Giroux, 1998), 5.

### Chapter 19. Fantasies Meet Reality

1. Mary Caroline Richards, *Centering in Pottery, Poetry, and the Person* (Middletown, CT: Wesleyan University Press, 1962).
2. Carolyn Brown, *Chance and Circumstance* (New York: Alfred A. Knopf, 2007).

## Chapter 27. Ups and Downs of the Dancers

1. Remy Charlip, author and illustrator, *Dress Up and Let's Have a Party* (New York: William R. Scott, 1956).
2. Remy Charlip and Jerry Joyner, *Thirteen* (New York: Parents' Magazine Press, 1975).

## Chapter 29. Separation Must Come

1. "Ochii Chornye," letter from Merce, 1991.

## Chapter 30. Family Wins

1. Merritt Lyndon Fernald and Alfred Charles Kinsey, revised by Reed C. Rollins, *Edible Wild Plants of Eastern North America* (New York: Harper and Brothers, 1943, 1958).

## Chapter 31. The Connection Holds

1. Review of Paul Taylor concert, *The Village Voice*, December 24, 1958.

## Chapter 32. Leaving New York, but Not Our Bond

1. *"The Saga of the Merce Cunningham Company"*—to the tune of *"The Frozen Logger"*—1970 by M. P-Simon

As I went out one evening
'Twas in a small cafe
A fifty-year-old waitress
These words to me did say:

"I knew you were a dancer
When I saw you passing by;
For no one but a dancer
Has such muscles in her thigh.

"My daughter, she was a dancer
And quite without a fuss
She danced around the country
In a Volkswagen Microbus.

"They piled in 6 dancers
2 musicians and a lighter of scenes
And nestled in beside them
Were the costumes and the screens.

"They often took their rest stops
When John Cage his phrase did call
So loud, so clear, so greedy,
'I SEE A GIANT PUFFBALL!'

"On Monday they danced in Ohio,
On Tuesday Pennsylvan-i-ay,
But in between they drove home
For they were too poor to stay.

"And everywhere reviewers
Would shout, 'What could be worse
Than music by John Cage
And choreography by Merce!'

"My daughter she had a baby
And left Cunningham and Cage
No sooner had she departed
Then they became the rage.

"Now though fame and honor follow them,
From here to the farthest shore,
You may be quite surprised to learn
They're still extremely poor."

And as that waitress finished,
And bid me a fond good-bye
I saw a tear squeezed outward
By the muscle in her eye.

And so I feel my duty
Is this history to tell
And the moral of the story is:
A dancer's life is Hell!

And if someone should ask me
To give a moral again
It's that a dancer's life is based
On wheat germ, yogurt, and Zen.

And if someone should ask me,
"Should I go see Merce dance?"
I'd say, "Why do as Merce does,
Toss a coin and take a chance."

### Chapter 33. Paris Calls Again

1. In 2012, Stephen Shelley began the annual BEAT Festival—Brooklyn Emerging Artists.
2. Elliot Caplan served as filmmaker in residence at the Merce Cunningham Dance Company from 1983 to 1998. His Cunningham films include *Points in Space* (1986), *Cage/Cunningham* (1991), and *Beach Birds for Camera* (1995).

### Chapter 34. Paris, November 1999

1. At that time, Alastair Macaulay was theater critic to the *Financial Times* and dance critic at the *Times Literary Supplement*, in London, England. Currently, he is the senior dance critic at the *New York Times*.
2. Trevor Carlson, new company manager at that time, later became the Cunningham company's executive director. Today, he is one of the five trustees of the Merce Cunningham Trust.

### Chapter 36. Merce Leaves, but His Legacy Is Forever

1. The final performances of the Cunningham company at the Park Avenue Armory were filmed and are available on DVD.

### Afterword

1. *Chance and Circumstance*, p. 3.
2. Merce Cunningham, "An American in Paris/ A Report from Merce Cunningham," pp. 131–32 of *Dance Observer* 16, no. 9 (November 1949), quoted on p. 53 of David Vaughan, *Merce Cunningham: Fifty Years.*
3. "Content is a Glimpse," Willem de Kooning interview with David Sylvester, recorded March 1960, The Willem de Kooning Foundation website, http://www.dekooning.org/documentation/words/content-is-a-glimpse.
4. Sontag, *Against Interpretation*, 1966, p. 14.
5. Patricia Lent, 2015, verbal introduction to The Merce Cunningham Trust's workshop showing of Cunningham's *Doubles*, in Studio 5 of New York City Center, formerly the New York City Center of Music and Drama.
6. This volume, p. 162.

# INDEX

Page numbers in *italics* refer to illustrations.

MARIANNE PREGER-SIMON, born in Brooklyn, New York, in 1929, was a founding member of the Merce Cunningham Dance Company, with which she danced between 1950 and 1958. During those years, she taught dance, drama, and world literature at the New Lincoln School in Manhattan. After leaving the stage to start a family, she received her Ed.D. from the University of Massachusetts at Amherst, led workshops in the United States and Canada in Values Clarification and Mother/Daughter Relationships, and has practiced psychotherapy for forty years. Married twice, she has birthed two children and was blessed with four more through marriage. Her life is now replete with grandchildren, great-grandchildren, and a large, lively, loving family.